DEVELOPING SUBJECT KNOWLEDGE IN DESIGN AND TECHNOLOGY:

SYSTEMS AND CONTROL

DEVELOPING SUBJECT KNOWLEDGE IN DESIGN AND TECHNOLOGY:

SYSTEMS AND CONTROL

Edited by
Gwyneth Owen-Jackson and John Myerson
at The Open University

Trentham Books
Stoke on Trent, UK and Sterling, USA

in association with

Trentham Books Limited

Westview House	22883 Quicksilver Drive
734 London Road	Sterling
Oakhill	VA 20166-2012
Stoke on Trent	USA
Staffordshire	
England ST4 5NP	

First published 2001

British Library Cataloguing-in-Publication Data
A catalogue record for this book is available from the British Library

ISBN: 1 85856 243 0

Cover picture supplied courtesy of Design and Technology Association
© DATA

Designed and typeset by Trentham Print Design Ltd., Chester and printed in Great Britain by Cromwell Press Ltd., Wiltshire.

Acknowledgements

This text draws heavily on The Open University course, T202 Analogue and digital electronics, and we want to thank the authors of that course for generously allowing their text to be used.

We also want to thank Brendan Henry who read through earlier drafts and helped us to get the work in order.

Contents

Introduction

The aim of this text is to develop your subject knowledge in systems and control. It discusses the systems approach and different types of systems. For those with no background knowledge at all in this area there is a section at the back of the book called 'Introduction to basic electronics', which covers basic facts about electronics and some of the main components.

Within the book elements in the National Curriculum for Design and Technology in England are addressed, as shown in the table below:

Key Stage 3
Knowledge and understanding of systems and control

Pupils should be taught:	Covered in:
a) to recognise inputs, processes and outputs in their own and existing products	Systems – identifying inputs and outputs
b) that complex systems can be broken down into sub-systems to make it easier to analyse them, and that each sub-system also has inputs, processes and outputs	Systems – identifying inputs and outputs types of systems Logic systems – Sequential logic
c) the importance of feedback in control systems	Systems – feedback – types of system
d) about (mechanical) electrical, electronic and pneumatic control systems, including the use of switches in electrical systems, sensors in electronic switching circuits...	Electronic systems Microprocessor control systems Computer control systems Logic systems Pneumatic systems (mechanical is not covered)
e) how different types of systems and sub-systems can be interconnected to achieve a particular function	Systems – selecting processes Logic systems
f) how to use electronics, microprocessors and computers to control systems, including the use of feedback	Electronic systems Microprocessor control systems Computer control systems Logic systems

Key Stage 4

Pupils should be taught:	Covered in:
a) the concepts of input, process and output, and the importance of feedback in controlling systems, including	Systems – identifying inputs and outputs feedback types of systems
i) how control systems and sub-systems can be designed, used and connected to different purposes	Systems – selecting processes Logic systems
ii) how feedback is incorporated into systems	Systems – types of systems
iii) how to analyse the performance of systems	Systems – analysing performance of systems

In addition, attention has been paid to meeting the knowledge specified as required to teach Design and Technology in *Minimum Competences for students to teach Design and Technology in secondary schools* (Design and Technology Association 1995).

Suggestions are given below for how you might use this text, but throughout you are seen as an active learner, engaging with the text and developing your knowledge and understanding.

Who is this book for?
This book is intended to be used as part of initial teacher training for Design and Technology, and may be used in a number of ways, for example:

• Pre-course, or at the very start of your course, you may choose to work through it all in one go

• At stages during your course (to suit your own time and needs) to satisfy subject audit requirements

How to use this book
It may be that you already have some knowledge of the areas covered in this text, and will only need to refer to some of the sections. Alternatively, you may be required to teach aspects of systems and control and so need to refer to the text to help you with planning lessons.

If you have little or no background knowledge the section 'Introduction to basic electronics' at the back of the book, gives basic terminology and describes some of the components used in systems and control. This introduction to electronics contains a lot of information and you are advised to work through it slowly. We suggest that you read and understand each part before moving on to the next. This may take some time but a thorough understanding will help you make better progress in other sections. You may also want to refer back to the 'Introduction to basic electronics' chapter as you work through sections of the book.

All the sections incorporate activities and questions to help you develop your understanding of systems and control. The book has been designed for self-study, but if it is possible you may wish to discuss these activities and questions with your professional tutor, school mentor or a design and technology teacher with knowledge of systems and control. This would help you to put the knowledge into an appropriate and relevant context.

Answers to questions are given at the back of the book.

This book will help you to teach systems and control to pupils at key stage 3. There will be time for you to further develop your knowledge and skills whilst you are teaching.

If there are other aspects of your subject knowledge which need to be developed, there are other books in this series which may help you.

Developing Subject Knowledge in Design and Technology – Food Technology

Developing Subject Knowledge – Structures

Developing Subject Knowledge – Developing, Planning and Communicating Ideas.

Systems

What are systems?

A system is the arrangement, set or collection of parts that are related and work together. Almost any device or natural object can be analysed as a system, but the systems approach is most widely applied to person management and control engineering. Control systems are connections of components that involve regulation or direction of themselves or other systems.

There are three basic elements of a system: input, output and a block or process that converts the input into a desirable output or response. Many systems have more than one input and output, and in addition there are unwanted inputs, such as interference, and unwanted outputs, such as 'noise' or waste heat.

Figure 1

How useful is a systems approach?

A systems approach can be used in two different ways: for designing new systems and for analysing existing ones. We use the 'language' of systems to describe the products and processes that we find around us. For example, we may be asked to identify the input, process and output elements of, say, a light detector or a simple food production line. In this way we develop a means of modelling and analysing existing systems. However, when these ideas are applied to everyday things, sometimes the model may look rather complicated in relation to what is quite a simple device. Using the language of systems for this purpose is valid only if it helps us to build up a vocabulary of systems terms.

An alternative use of a systems approach is to help with designing. In this case the systems language is used to inform our design choices. Such a language is especially useful when the systems are complex (or relatively complex). Complex systems, from power stations to video recorders, are designed by applying the systems approach in an organised way to novel situations. Thus if a moisture sensor is being designed using a transistor driver circuit, we could design at the level of the system, even though we may not know the details of how it worked. All we need to know is what the transistor driver does with the input. Similarly we might work on elements (sub-systems) of a larger project such as designing food batch-production procedures to produce pizzas.

Identifying inputs and outputs

Identifying outputs from systems is generally straightforward, as the purpose of the system is usually clear. Identifying inputs is more difficult. Take the example of a personal CD player. The output is obviously sound (speech or music), but what are the inputs? The process certainly won't work without batteries to provide electrical power; most systems need some form of energy input. Looking at the device as a control system, it must have a stimulus or excitation to produce the required output of sound. This input is the (digital) information on the CD. So the system diagram looks like figure 2. The details of the process are not important at this stage. There are of course a number of other systems in the CD such as the motor speed control and the logic that controls the order in which songs are heard.

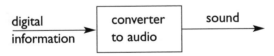

Figure 2: Simplified diagram of CD Player system

Question 1

What are the inputs and outputs of these systems (and their sub-systems where applicable):

1   A wall switch operating a room light.

2   An analogue voltmeter (one with a rotating pointer).

3   A washing machine

4   A bicycle

Boundaries need to be set to systems to enable them to be analysed easily, in particular, whether human operators can be regarded as part of the system or not. In the example of the radio volume control, the human acts as a regulator of the system, responding to the volume level of the output and adjusting the input to suit.

This is a simple example of feedback, which is an essential part of a closed-loop system (see below), and is designed to make the system self-regulating.

There are two basic types of control system, open loop and closed loop systems.

Open loop describes a system in which the building blocks connect together in simple linear way, and where a particular input produces a particular output.

Closed loop describes a system which has a feedback. Feedback involves the use of a sensor to detect changes at the output and to feed information back to the control device, which may modify the output as a consequence.

Feedback

The term 'feedback' has now become quite a common word in general vocabulary, so that it has lost some of the more precise meaning that engineers gave it when it was first coined. In control systems the output of a system is compared with the desired output. If there is a difference between the two, feedback is used to ensure that this information is connected in to the system in such a way that the output is brought back towards its intended value. This is usually called **negative feedback** because the correction is applied by subtraction.

The 'system' containing the feedback can be almost anything. For instance, the process of driving a car down a road is a feedback process. The output (the position and velocity of the car) is sensed by the driver and compared with his or her expectations. Corrections are then made to the settings of steering wheel, accelerator, brake etc., to ensure that the output conforms to the intentions of the driver. In a control system like this there are two kinds of input: the primary input is the driver's intentions, the secondary inputs are the petrol, air, brake linings, etc. The process is one of comparing the output with the primary input and then adjusting the system (including the secondary inputs) to correct any errors.

You can see the principle of how beneficial properties from feedback come about by considering a commonly used negative feedback system; the thermostatically controlled central heating system, illustrated in figure 3.

In such a system the thermostat is set to the desired output temperature (the primary input), and a boiler is installed which is capable of providing enough heat to achieve this. Obviously the boiler will have a greater heating capability than is needed most of the time. When the temperature in the room

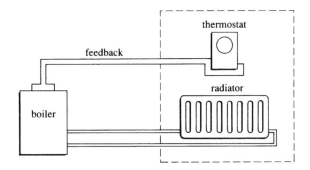

Figure 3: A central-heating
system showing the feedback
from the thermostat to the
boiler. The thermostat compares
the actual temperature with the
intended temperature and
causes the boiler to be switched
on or off appropriately

gets too hot the boiler is switched off, and when it gets too cold in the room the boiler is switched on again. The 'error' in the output temperature is controlling the secondary inputs of gas and air for example. So, as you would expect, the system keeps the room at approximately the intended temperature.

It does this despite fluctuations in the outside temperature, variations in the use of the room, the addition of extra heating, such as an open fire, variations in the gas or oil pressure supplying the boiler and even some loss of efficiency in the boiler. In other words the system gives a 'predictable and flat response' despite 'distortion' produced by variations in the boiler output, noise or interference within the feedback loop, and variations in the load on the system caused by usage and the weather.

It is also possible to produce systems that are often referred to as 'positive feedback'. In such systems any error is reinforced rather than reduced by the feedback signal. Vicious circles are such systems. A central-heating system connected the wrong way round so that too high a temperature turns the boiler on, would provide an example of this.

Inertial lag and stability

The lag or delay in a feedback system is the most likely cause of a system failing to achieve an intended goal. A central heating system can oscillate around the target temperature due to the effect of lags or delays in the boiler, pipes and thermostat. If it takes a long time for the boiler to be switched on when the temperature is too low, or to be switched off when it is too high, then the temperature may fluctuate uncomfortably. If on the other hand the lag is too short, the system may turn on and off frequently as it 'hunts' above and below the required temperature.

Types of systems

Figure 4 shows a simple system as a schematic diagram with the basic elements.

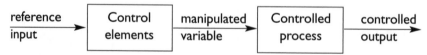

Figure 4: Schematic diagram of an open loop system

This is known as **open-loop system** because the output is independent of the input. The output from such a system may or may not conform to the specified response from a given input. A simple example is the volume control on a radio. The position of the control knob may indicate a medium volume output, but the actual output is dependent on a number of factors including the power of the audio amplifier, but also whether the system is working correctly. This type of system is partially calibrated by the manufacturer who decides the range of volume required by the consumer, but the actual adjustment is left to the user. However, open-loop systems have two advantages:

1   They are generally more stable

2   The system can be calibrated to establish accurate working, that is, numbers or limits can be given to the inputs to assign a relationship with desired outputs.

Closed-loop systems use feedback to sample the output and compare it with the input so that appropriate control action can be applied. Additional elements are required to show this in schematic form. In some texts the Controlled Process is called the Plant (as in machinery, not the growing type!). The feedback loop is combined with the reference input at the *summing point*. The minus sign denotes negative feedback (the control signal is subtracted) and the plus sign denotes positive feedback.

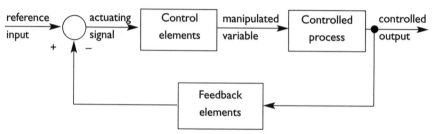

Figure 5: Schematic diagram of a closed-loop system with feedback

Although the stability of systems is usually defined by reference to mathematical analysis, we can use a simple definition. A stable system will stay in a steady state unless excited by an external source, and will return to rest when the external source is removed. The time taken to effect the control from feedback has an effect on the variation of the output. In the central heating scenario above a typical thermostat does not switch off immediately on temperature rise, so there is a lag in time before the system responds and turns the boiler off.

Activity 1

Use a thermometer to record the air temperature near a central heating thermostat (or an electric convector heater) every 30 seconds for a half an hour or so. If you can, record when the thermostat switches (you should hear a click). Draw a graph from the measurements. What do you notice about the variation in temperature? See the discussion below on the performance of systems.

NB If you have access to datalogging equipment, this will make the recording automatic.

You probably found that the operation of the thermostat came well after the set temperature and that the temperature did not drop immediately. The thermostat probably came on again below the set temperature. In other words, there was a lag between temperature change and control of the heat source.

Systems with negative feedback tend to be stable because the control correction is subtracted, whereas positive feedback systems tend to be unstable. A common example of instability is when a public address system is being used and a microphone picks up sound from the loudspeaker. This sound is amplified by the system and returns to the loudspeaker to be amplified further thus causing the well-known high frequency squeal.

Question 2

Draw schematic block diagrams showing the feedback loops and control elements of these systems:

1   *Central heating with a thermostat*

2   *Water tank with float valve*

3   *Electric toaster with bread colour detector*

4   *Electric motor with rotation counter*

Often systems can be further analysed into sub-systems. The 'process' block (between the input and output) can be re-interpreted as containing a number of other systems. An example of this is an electricity power plant. The main system has fuel (coal, oil, etc.) as its input and electricity as its output. The process can be broken down into a chain of sub-processes that involve the production of steam from burning the fuel, the reaction of the turbines to produce kinetic energy and the electromagnetic induction that produces electricity. Each of these sub-systems has its own inputs, processes and outputs, and each sub-system can be analysed separately. In fact, complex systems usually are broken down into their constituent sub-systems when an analysis is required

Selecting processes

When the purpose of a product is established the outputs are usually clear, but the inputs are more difficult to determine. This partly depends on the type of system required. If, for example, movement is required as an output it may be that a mechanical system is required with a mechanical input. The gear system on a bicycle, which controls the effort applied and the output speed, is an obvious example of a mechanical system. However, if we were designing a cooling system for a room the choice of system is not so clear cut. The choice could range from a refrigeration plant to an extractor fan. Whichever system is chosen, there is a need for energy and control inputs. In both these cases the control input could be the signal from a thermostat.

Table 1 is an attempt to show the range of processes available for particular control functions.

Table I Control processes and possible systems

Control Process	System		
	Electrical/electronic	**Mechanical**	**Pneumatic**
On/off	Switch	Clutch	Valve
Speed control	Variable resistor Timer/Pulse generator	Friction brake	Throttle/ restrictor valve
One way flow or movement	Diode (and light-emitting diode)	Ratchet Worm & worm-wheel	Non-return valve
Time delay	Capacitor	Damper/dashpot	Restrictor & reservoir

Often the output is one type of system and the input is another. In these cases a transducer or sensor may be needed on the input to change the effect from one type to another, for example a mechanical input may need to control an electrical device.

To transfer control from one process type to another requires an interface. For example, an electrical switch to control the opening of a door by means of pneumatics. A solenoid valve will convert an electrical voltage to the flow of air to a piston. Interfaces are also required in electronic devices because the current output of one circuit or device (such as a computer) may be insufficient to drive the next stage.

Typical interface devices are shown in table 2.

Table 2 Interfaces

Input from	Output to:		
	Electronic/electrical	Mechanical	Pneumatic
Electronic/electrical	Transistor driver Relay Opto-isolator	Solenoid Motor Servo	Solenoid valve
Mechanical	Microswitch Reed switch	Crank and slider Cam Rack and pinion	Roller trip valve
Pneumatic	Diaphragm valve with microswitch	Piston	Pressure sensitive valve Air-operated valve

Analysing performance of systems

In the open-loop arrangement, the goal is achieved by choosing or operating the system by specifying the input conditions for a certain desired output. If we want a greater illumination then we choose a higher wattage bulb; if we want a lighter or darker shade of toast we must alter the toaster and wait. If we set the level incorrectly (as usual!) then we must guess again and have another try. The degree to which the output coincides with the goal is called the performance of the system. In open-loop control poor performance means you have either selected the system components incorrectly or adjusted them wrongly. To get it right you must start again.

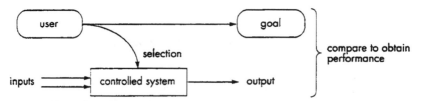

Figure 6: Open-loop control in which the user selects or initially adjusts the system. No feedback is involved. 'Performance' is the success with which the 'output' achieves the 'goal'.

For a closed-loop system the goal is an input to the system, known as the reference input. In this case, if the performance is unsatisfactory because the difference between the output and the goal is too large, then the system can be adjusted to improve matters. (See figure 7 below)

First we must identify the user and then concentrate on the goal of the system. Going back to the example of a central heating system, the user who concerns us in this case is the person in whose house the system is installed. The householder's goal is to achieve a particular room temperature – whatever the outside temperature. So the output of the system is the room temperature the system actually achieves, and the system performance is a function of the difference between the intended temperature and the actual temperature. The user sets the intended temperature, so this setting is the reference input to the system.

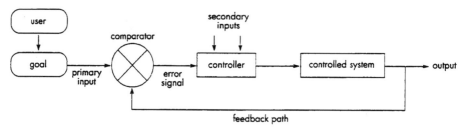

Figure 7: Closed loop control. System performance is measured in the comparator and the controller uses the resulting error signal to make an adjustment.

(Note particularly that the heat from the radiators is not the system output. The heat output from the boiler and radiators is part of the controlled system, by means of which the room temperature is achieved. Heat and temperature are not quite the same things. Heat gives rise to a change in temperature.)

Let us now summarise how the central heating system works once everything is connected up. First you set the goal by adjusting the knob on the thermostat. A 'thermometer' in the thermostat compares the room temperature with the required temperature. It then operates a switch at or near the target temperature, so that when the room temperature is too *high* the boiler is turned off and when the room temperature is too *low* the boiler is turned on. This arrangement ensures that the output, the actual room temperature, is kept close to the goal, namely the intended room temperature. In other words, the *error* between the goal and the output is kept small. The boiler is switched on and off at fairly regular intervals so that the average heat input into the room just balances the loss of heat through windows, walls, doors etc. The actual temperature fluctuates a little but keeps fairly close to the target temperature.

Electronics systems

Digital electronics is concerned with electrical systems made up of a series of switches. These switches are, in themselves, very simple; they are either on or off, nothing else will do. The complication arises in the way that they are switched, or what the input requirements are for the switch to operate.

A computer is a very complicated digital circuit. It is made up from hundreds of components, that are each very simple switching units connected together to form the full complicated switching unit called a computer.

Digital electronics are used in many items around us. The digital watch and calculator were two of the first widely used digital devices. Today an increasing number of electrical and mechanical devices have become digitized. The mechanical switching unit on a washing machine has now been replaced by a very small, reliable, low-cost digital electrical control unit.

The design and use of electronics systems is an example of the value of using 'know-how' rather than 'know-why' in technological activities. It is a goal-oriented approach that is an essential ingredient of the successful use of electronics in designing. Rather than focusing on any scientific understanding of the way in which the devices and circuits work, the emphasis is on the functional aspects of the electronic devices and circuits that are to be used.

The design criteria might be:

- What should the electronics system do?

- What operating conditions, e.g. power supply requirements, does it need to work?

- Will the device stand up to rigours of use in its intended environment?

- How much will it cost to make and run?

- What characteristics of the device are better for this design than other similar devices?

- Will it be safe and easy to use?

- Can the components required be obtained easily?

- Will it be acceptable, culturally and economically, to the people in the community in which it is to be used?

To a technologist, meeting these functional and contextual criteria are as important a consideration as knowing why the electronic devices used work in the way they do.

The emphasis on function and context rather than theory and fundamentals may be misleading, seeming to lack opportunities for rigorous thought. However, the design and assembly of circuits and systems for specific purposes requires knowledge and understanding at the operational level. These operating precepts are just as demanding intellectually as the concepts such as electrical conductivity and potential. An example or two will make these points clearer.

Designing electronic systems

The input, process, output blocks can represent an electronics system. It is an assembly of functional electronic building blocks that are connected together to achieve a particular purpose, e.g. sounding an alarm when smoke is in the air.

Typical electronic 'building' blocks are shown in table 1.

Table 1 (Examples of electronic building blocks)		
Input	**Process**	**Output**
switch (mechanical and semiconductor)	amplifier	light-emitting diode
microphone	comparator	7 segment display loudspeaker
light-dependent resistor	oscillator	meter
thermistor	counter	light bulb
smoke detector	transistor driver	buzzer

Thus the input building block of a fire alarm could be a smoke detector. Its processor building block might comprise a comparator to switch on an audio frequency oscillator when the smoke level detected by the sensor has reached a pre-set danger point followed, perhaps, by an amplifier. The detector's output building block would be a small loudspeaker or piezoelectric device to generate an audio frequency sound when signals are received from the oscillator.

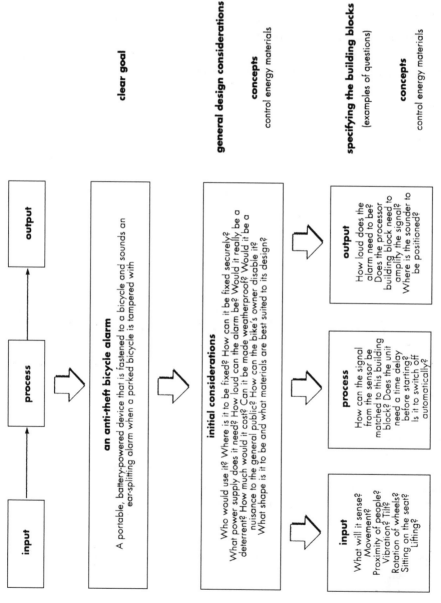

Figure 1: The linked building blocks of an electronic system and some of the technological criteria and concepts to be considered

input → **process** → **output**

an anti-theft bicycle alarm

A portable, battery-powered device that is fastened to a bicycle and sounds an ear-splitting alarm when a parked bicycle is tampered with

clear goal

initial considerations

Who would use it? Where is it to be fixed? How can it be fixed? How can it be fixed securely? What power supply does it need? How loud can the alarm be? Would it really be a deterrent? How much would it cost? Can it be made weatherproof? Would it be a nuisance to the general public? How can the bike's owner disable it? What shape is it to be and what materials are best suited to its design?

general design considerations

concepts
control energy materials

input
What will it sense?
Movement?
Proximity of people?
Vibration? Tilt?
Rotation of wheels?
Sitting on the seat?
Lifting?

process
How can the signal from the sensor be matched to this building block? Does the unit need a time delay before starting? Is it to switch off automatically?

output
How loud does the alarm need to be? Does the processor building block need to amplify the signal? Where is the sounder to be positioned?

specifying the building blocks
(examples of questions)

concepts
control energy materials

Let's look at a more complex problem. An anti-theft warning device is required to clip onto a bicycle and provide an ear-piercing sound if the bicycle is about to be stolen, i.e. it is a portable device to be used by an individual. First and foremost, there needs to be a clear specification of what the system is to do, see figure 1.

Second, there needs to be a consideration of the environment it is to be used in, not just the physical environment (e.g. wet, dusty, hot, cold or dry) but the human environment too.

- Who is to use it

- What is it to look like – its shape, colour, size and so on;

- How it is to be used, e.g. whether fixed to the wheels, handlebars or forks;

- How much it is to cost to make and to sell;

- Whether the user needs to have any technical skills to use it;

- Is it acceptable to the public who may not want additional noise in their environment – though if they don't it defeats the purpose of the device!

Only after these criteria are established through appropriate research is the selection of the functional building blocks possible that will enable a prototype system to be made which meets the criteria. There are several concepts that arise in this analysis of need. For example, in terms of energy there is a consideration of the power supply requirements. In terms of the process:

- How can the device control the sound long and loud enough to alert attention?

- Is it to have an automatic cut-out?

- What is to be the operating principle of the sensor that first detects the movement of the bicycle?

In terms of materials, consideration need to be given to cost, ruggedness, waterproofing and design of the casing for the unit.

When it comes to the manufacture of the anti-theft bicycle alarm, however, the technical factors to be considered are more than simply selecting appropriate input, process and output devices, plugging them together and expecting the system to work. What is most often missed in designing electronic systems is the need to consider the requirements that enable each building block to respond to the signal it receives and send an appropriate signal to the building block that follows it. The concept being highlighted here is called **matching**. This is more complex, but computer software is available which will give the design for a printed circuit board combining the contributory functional blocks. For example, for the anti-theft bicycle alarm different sensors such as a tilt switch, vibration switch, magnetic switch, or a capacitance switch produce different signals and these differences should be recognised and examined using a multimeter or an oscilloscope. The signal produced by the sensor determines the choice of the processor building block, which might be a comparator, or a counter or an amplifier. And similarly with the output building block that needs to respond to the signal produced by the processor building block.

Microprocessor control systems

A microprocessor is an integrated circuit with a large number of components in one chip. It is controlled by a set of binary instruction usually stored in a memory chip. There are microprocessors that are dedicated to specific tasks, such as providing clock pulses and output waveforms, but most are controlled by whatever instructions are in memory. Because the memory contents can be changed the microprocessor is very versatile. The instructions are written in a binary machine code, which is difficult to programme so a higher level language was devised called assembly language. This consists of simple abbreviations (such as LD for load, JP for jump) which can be input from a keyboard. Assembly language has to be interpreted by a program stored in memory before control instructions are sent to the microprocessor. Higher level languages such as BASIC (Beginners All purpose Symbolic Instruction Code) go one step further from machine code so that instructions can be written in 'almost English', but these require more interpretation for the microprocessor. One way around this problem is to write the program in BASIC on a computer, use software to compile the instructions in machine code and send them to the memory chip by a hard-wired connection. Once programmed the microprocessor can operate independently of the computer. To make a microprocessor do something sensible in the real world it needs an interface that will receive control inputs and give output instructions to control devices. The complete system is shown in figure 1.

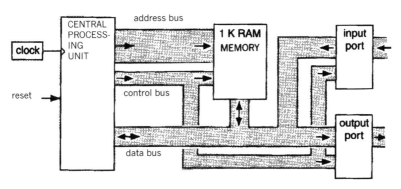

Figure 1: Block diagram of a microprocessor

A microprocessor designed for systems control is the Peripheral Interface Controller (PIC). It has a reduced set of instructions and can be programmed from a computer. A number of manufacturers make development kits for this device with all the links for computers and output devices (see the website appendix).

There is also a number of other microprocessor devices. *Programmable Logic Devices* (PLDs) are standard, off-the-shelf user programmable integrated circuits used to implement custom logic functions. A typical device might have 8 inputs and 8 outputs and contain over 100 logic gates on one chip. The PLD therefore replaces a large number of individual logic gates and can be programmed so that the *input* responds in a particular way to the *inputs*. Again there is computer software available to programme these devices.

Computer control systems

Many small-scale devices such as TV remote controls, washing machines, microwave ovens have dedicated microprocessor controllers, but for versatility and ease of experimental work the standard personal computer can be used for control. With the addition of an interface that can handle larger currents than the computer, a large range of input and output devices can be used. Provided the voltage and current output of the interface matches the device, bulbs, motors, solenoids, buzzers, etc can be plugged in. Most interfaces also have digital inputs, i.e. various types of switches can be connected directly. Some interfaces also have analogue inputs that will accept various sensors. The computer will then indicate a value for the sensor input between 0% and 100%.

Programming methods are of four main types:

1   Using a computer language such as BASIC

2   Using a high level language such as LOGO and its extensions

3   Using flow charts

4   Using ladder-logic icons.

Programming in BASIC

Although this is not difficult it does require some knowledge of BASIC which is not at all forgiving if words are misspelled. Procedures are used to contain sub-programs that can be tested individually before running the whole program. The output and input addresses must be known. Logic statements deal with inputs because the inputs are given as a denary number representing a series of 0s and 1s.

As an example, the old BBC computer had an output/input port at address 65120, and a control address at 65122. The port has 8 bits or connections that can be configured as inputs or outputs.

So to test an input on bit 7 the program might look like:

10 ?65122 = 15   (switches first four bits on as outputs)

20 IF (?65120 AND 128) = 128   (checks to see if the input is on bit 7 by
THEN PROClights ELSE 20   using AND logic, if true program jumps to
                                      the 'lights' procedure or else checks again)

As you can see the programming is a little involved and there are easier ways
of doing it.

Programming in LOGO

A number of control programs are available that use a set of instructions
based on the Logo computer language. The simplified language includes
words such as SWITCHON, SWITCHOFF, WAIT and REPEAT which are
fairly obvious. To test for an input on bit 7 as above would look like:

WAIT UNTIL (INPUTON? 7) THEN
LIGHTS   (where LIGHTS is a defined
                                 procedure)

Which is a little simpler. However, both BASIC and LOGO are linear
programs that can branch if certain conditions are met, but two procedures
cannot run simultaneously.

Programming with flowcharts

There are two main advantages with flowchart programming. Firstly, more
than one flowchart procedure can run at the same time and secondly, the
programming is more visual so that the possible routes of control instructions
can be traced.

Figure 1 shows what the flowchart
would look like for testing bit 7. The
program takes care of the output
address etc. provided the options are
set correctly at the outset. Most flow
chart programs will also allow an on-
screen simulation of the control.
Coloured areas of the screen are
switched on or off in relation to the
required output. Editing is graphically.

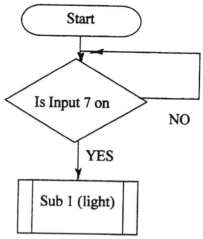

Figure 1: Flowchart programming

Programming with ladder logic

Ladder logic is a concept that allows parallel processing, i.e. several control events to happen at the same time. Each control function is like a rung of a ladder with the starting connection on the left 'upright' and the output on the right. An example is shown in figure 2.

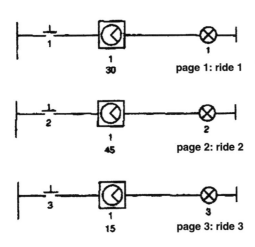

The basis of the icons used is the same as the systems approach outlined in another section, i.e. input, process and output, and has similarities with sequential electronic logic.

The application of logic to inputs is visually similar to the use of switches in series for AND and in parallel for OR.

Figure 2: Ladder logic programming

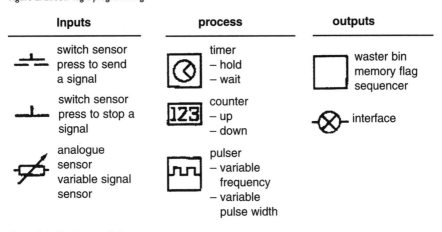

Inputs	process	outputs
switch sensor press to send a signal	timer – hold – wait	waster bin memory flag sequencer
switch sensor press to stop a signal	counter – up – down	interface
analogue sensor variable signal sensor	pulser – variable frequency – variable pulse width	

Figure 3: Ladder logic symbols

Logic systems

Digital signals and logic circuits

There are two kinds of simple waveform that are commonly used to analyse the behaviour of circuits. One kind is the sinusoidal waveform used to test amplifiers and is called an analogue signal. The electricity changes in step with the sound it is representing and so moves up and down, i.e. it is 'analogous' to the sound wave. The other kind is the digital waveform in which the information is carried by patterns of two voltage levels, usually referred to as patterns of 1s and 0s, as illustrated in figure 1(a) and called binary or digital signals or waveforms. The binary digital signal in this case can be described as 0101100101110. The voltage at any instant at any point in a circuit is considered to be either one value or the other (e.g. 5V or 0V) and the transitions between the two voltages are regarded as being so brief as to be instantaneous. So in order to receive a digital signal accurately and decide

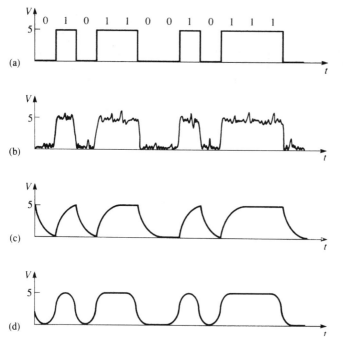

Figure 1:A binary digital signal (a) in ideal form (b) affected by noise; (c) and (d) different forms of frequency distortion

24

whether a 1 or a 0 is being transmitted it is only necessary to be able to recognise whether a voltage over the short period of each digital pulse is greater than or less than a particular threshold value. Thus, even with the noisy or distorted waveforms of Figures 1(b), (c) and (d) it is possible for a detector to distinguish without error that the signal transmitted is the same as that of figure 1(a). There is a limit to how much distortion and noise there can be before errors begin to arise, but binary signals are clearly much less sensitive to noise than analogue ones.

Digital circuits are of two kinds. One kind is concerned with the transmission of digital waveforms from a transmitter to a receiver. For such purposes amplifiers are needed to overcome the losses along the line. For digital signals the circuits have only to be capable of receiving a sequence of distorted and diminished pulses and regenerating an undistorted replica of the input signal for transmission further down the line. Such amplifiers are called 'regenerative repeaters' rather than simply amplifiers or digital amplifiers, because they clean up the signal as well as amplifying it.

The second type of digital circuit is called a **logic circuit** and its function is to combine two or more inputs and create one or more outputs that are logical functions of the inputs. Logic circuits, such as those in calculators and computers, are assemblies of basic logic elements called logic gates. The design of digital circuits is mainly concerned with how to assemble a number of gates so that the assembly will perform a specified function, such as doing arithmetic, giving digital displays of letters and numbers or controlling an industrial process by changing the settings of machines in a workshop.

Perhaps the simplest example of a logic circuit is the two- or three-switch arrangement that most people have in their houses for controlling the first floor light from the ground and first floors. The specification for such a system is simply that changing the state of either switch, whatever its existing state, must change the state of the light. Whether the light is on or off, each switch, when it is operated, must *change* the state of the light.

The usual way of achieving the two-switch arrangement is shown in figure 2. It makes use of two 'change-over' switches, A and B, with two wires running

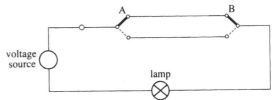

Figure 2: Circuits to control a first-floor landing light from either of two switches: using change over switches.

Figure 3: (Circuits to control a first-floor landing light from either of two switches: using on-off switches and a control box

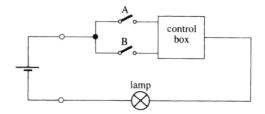

between them. It is easy to see that this will achieve the stated specification. Change the state of either switch and the lamp will change state.

Now suppose that a DC supply was being used instead of the AC mains supply and that only on-off switches were to be used, rather than the change-over ones of figure 2. It would be necessary to use an arrangement like that shown in figure 3.

The circuit in the control box would have to be a digital circuit with two inputs and one output, which would perform the same function as that of figure 2. That is, the output would either be 1 or 0, representing, in this case, the presence or absence of a voltage applied to the lamp. The question is what circuit should be put in the box?

Table 1 shows the first step in the design process: the compiling of a *truth table* to represent the required performance. The first two columns show the possible sequence of switching operations. Beginning with both switches A and B in the ON state and the lamp OFF, the specification demands that when any input switch changes state the output always changes too. By using the transitions from one row of the table to the next to represent the possible switch *changes*, the next three rows of the table can be written in. It is easy to see that every possible sequence of switching steps is represented in this table – reading either upwards or downwards.

A	B	lamp
ON	ON	OFF
ON	OFF	ON
OFF	OFF	OFF
OFF	ON	ON

Table 1

Table 2 shows the same information using 1s and 0s to represent the two states of both the switches and the lamp.

A	B	lamp
1	1	0
1	0	1
0	0	0
0	1	1

Table 2

An inspection of Table 2 shows that the circuit in the control box must give an output of 1 when the two inputs differ, and give an output of 0 when the two inputs are the same. This is the specified logic function for this application; and the particular logic gate that performs it is called an Exclusive OR gate (XOR gate). The circuit diagram, including a symbol for an XOR gate is shown in figure 4.

Figure 4: Circuits to control a first-floor landing light from either of two switches: using an Exclusive-OR gate as the control circuit

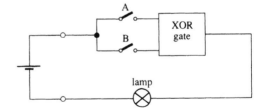

Now consider a somewhat more complicated circuit, which is needed when there are three switches controlling one lamp. Figure 5 shows a three-switch arrangement using mechanical switches.

Figure 5: Circuits to control a first-floor landing light from any one of three switches: using two changeover switches and a reversing switch

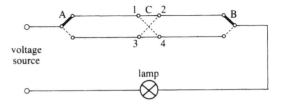

The middle switch C is a specially designed switch, sometimes called a reversing switch, which either connects pin 1 to pin 2, and pin 3 to pin 4, or else connects pin 1 to pin 4 and pin 2 to pin 3. Figure 6 shows the logic circuit containing two XOR gates (and a DC supply) and Table 3 is its corresponding truth table.

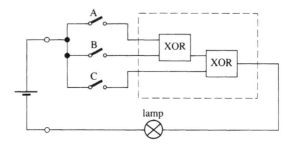

Figure 6: Circuits to control a first-floor landing light from any one of three switches: using three on-off switches and two XOR gates in the control box

A	B	C	lamp
I	I	I	I
I	I	0	0
I	0	0	I
I	0	I	0
0	0	0	0
0	I	0	I
0	I	0	I
0	I	I	0

Table 3

Activity I

Remembering that an XOR gate only gives an output of I when its inputs are different from each other, check that the circuit of figure 6 fulfils the required specification. It's best to decide on the order in which you are going to do this before you start.

Look at inputs A and B first to one XOR gate (table 2) gives this result. Then combine this with input C. Another way to look at it is to consider each row of the three inputs; changing one of them only should change the state of the output.

Digital circuits that perform logical operations can usefully be divided into two categories, called **combinational logic** circuits and **sequential logic** circuits. Combinational circuits are those whose output is an immediate function of its inputs, as was the case with two- and three-switch arrangements for controlling the first-floor landing light. Sequential circuits are circuits whose outputs depend, in addition, on previous inputs to the circuit, and which therefore also include some memory or storage elements. Computers are obvious examples of the latter. They can store a great deal of data, and will produce an output that depends on both immediate instructions as well as on stored information.

Digital circuits were intended originally only for use as control signals for switches and relays, as, for example, in telephone exchanges and lifts. Such circuits were originally called 'switching circuits' for obvious reasons, but although the name is no longer very appropriate for some of the more recent applications, it has remained in use as an alternative name for this kind of digital circuit. Since the 1950s digital signals, because of their inherently greater freedom from the effects of noise and distortion, have come more and more into use as a means of handling analogue signals too, such as speech or music or the outputs of measuring instruments. To achieve this it is obviously necessary for there to be a process of 'analogue-to-digital conversion', or 'A-D conversion', together with the complementary process of 'D-A conversion'.

Combinational logic systems

You are asked to design a device, an interlock, that prevents a machine from operating by disconnecting the power supply to the machine. So, when the machine is switched on, it will only operate if various safety conditions are satisfied. For example, an automatic lathe may require three conditions to be satisfied before the ON/OFF switch causes the workpiece in the lathe to rotate. These are:

Conditions

• The workpiece is in position.

• Adequate lubricant is available.

• A safety guard is in position.

The function of the interlock is to check the conditions to see whether they are satisfied, and if they are *all* satisfied the power will be connected to the machine. The three conditions can therefore be regarded as the inputs to the interlock. The output of the interlock is its ability to select whether the power is connected to the machine or not.

There are four steps to the design of a digital interlock system:

1 Express the possible input conditions and output requirements in binary form.

2 Tabulate the relationship between the input conditions and the required output.

3 Choose transducers that will convert the actual conditions into electrical signals that can be handled by digital electronic circuits.

4   Find or design an electronic device with electrical inputs and outputs that match those of the transducers and in which the inputs and outputs are related in the way expressed in Step 2.

Step 1: Binary inputs and outputs

If the input conditions and the output requirements are to be expressed in binary form, they must be phrased so that there are only two possibilities in each case. These alternatives are then labelled 0 and 1. There is usually more than one way of phrasing the conditions to give clear alternative possibilities. For example, a condition required of the work-piece can be expressed as the answer to any of the following questions:

'Is the workpiece in position?'

Answer: YES or NO;

or 'Where is the workpiece? Is it in or out of position?'

Answer: IN or OUT;

or as the statement 'The workpiece is in position.'

Answer: TRUE or FALSE.

The alternatives YES, IN or TRUE describe the same state of affairs, and could be represented by 1. The alternatives NO, OUT or FALSE would then be represented by 0. However, this is a matter of choice – the important things are that the condition should be carefully phrased so that there are only two possible choices, and that the decision as to which shall be represented by 1 and which by 0 should be clearly understood.

There are many other situations where two clear alternatives are possible. A lamp can be ON or OFF, a toggle switch can be UP or DOWN, a machine can STOP or GO, and so on. These are situations where the alternatives can easily be translated into the binary symbols 0 and 1. If the situations are expressed as statements that can only be TRUE or FALSE, this links the world of practical affairs with the formal language of logic.

When we are designing we allow for both possibilities, so we need a way of stating that the condition is relevant but we do not know what that condition is. To do this we use the idea of a *variable*. The three input conditions to be satisfied by the interlock can be labelled as A, B and C. The output requirement of the interlock can be labelled as P. Each variable can take on either of the two binary values, 0 or 1, each of which represents a particular situation.

Variable	Value	Situation represented
A	1	Workpiece in position
	0	Workpiece not in position
B	1	Adequate lubricant available
	0	Adequate lubricant not available
C	1	Safety guard in position
	0	Safety guard not in position
P	1	Mains switch turns machine on
	0	Mains switch disconnected

We can then say that when A = 1, for example, the workpiece is in position. This is the notation of **Boolean algebra**, named after the nineteenth century mathematician George Boole. A, B, C and P are described as Boolean variables, which can take one of only two values, 0 and 1. You will be relieved to know that Boolean arithmetic is not developed here, so you will have to refer to other texts for further explanation!

Even quantities like a liquid level or voltage can be given a description that can be represented by the symbols 0 or 1. A liquid level or voltage can be said to be HIGH or LOW in relation to some reference value.

There is a problem in practical systems about values near a dividing line and uncertainty about measurements. This point is relevant to the second of the interlock conditions, B, which is not satisfactorily phrased as it stands. What does '*adequate lubricant available*' mean? It can either refer to the *flow* of lubricant over the work, required to be more than a specified number of litres per second or to the *level* of lubricant in a storage tank, required to be above some specified minimum. By setting these specified quantities sufficiently above the anticipated danger levels, a safety margin could be provided, allowing for uncertainty about the measurement of the flow or level.

Question 1
How could the input condition C (safety guard in position) and the output requirement P (mains switch turns machine on) be expressed in words to provide clear binary alternatives?

Once the conditions have been given binary alternatives, the designer can then move on to the second step.

Step 2: The input-output relationship

The required relationship between the inputs A, B and C and the output P can now be stated in a table which will form the specification for the required interlock. Each possible combination of input conditions must be considered in turn. Thus, if the workpiece is not in position (A = 0), there is not adequate lubricant (B = 0) and the safety guard is *not* in position (C = 0), we require that the mains switch should not turn the machine on (P = 0). This can be written as:

A	B	C	P
0	0	0	0

If only one or two of the input conditions are satisfied, we still require that P = 0. Thus, if the workpiece is in position and there is adequate lubricant, but the safety guard is not in position, this can be written as:

A	B	C	P
1	1	0	0

For the purpose of specifying the interlock the order of the columns labelled A, B and C does not matter.

Question 2

What does this truth table mean?

A	B	C	P
0	0	1	0

The mains switch should only turn the machine on when *all three* input conditions are suitable; that is, when *A*, *B* and *C* all have the value of 1.

A	B	C	P
1	1	1	1

A *complete* description of the required interlock involves a complete list of all possible combinations of inputs with the required output. If any of the input combinations gives the wrong output the interlock will not be working properly. You will see from the table that with three input conditions there are eight possible input combinations, only one of which gives *P* = 1.

A	B	C	P
0	0	0	0
0	0	1	0
0	1	0	0
0	1	1	0
1	0	0	0
1	0	1	0
1	1	0	0
1	1	1	1

If a system has two inputs, they can be combined four ways, namely 00, 01, 10 and 11. Three inputs, as above, can be combined in eight different ways, each row of the truth table corresponding to one of the input combinations. This ability to combine the inputs in different ways is the basis for calling the type of circuits that ultimately implement the truth table **combinational circuits**.

There would be no change in the interpretation of the truth table if the rows were rearranged. However, it is usual to write truth tables with the possible input combinations arranged in the systematic way shown here to avoid missing any, so it pays to learn the system. If you are already familiar with binary numbers you should be able to see that the rows in the truth table (just the inputs) can be interpreted as three-digit binary numbers. The rows are then written in order starting from 000 at the top to 111 at the bottom.

Question 3
What are the 16 different combinations that can be made with four binary variables? Make a list of them and then arrange them in the systematic way described above.

Step 3: Electrical logic levels
The two steps taken so far have nothing to do with electronics. The conditions have simply been expressed in binary form and the required relationship between inputs and outputs expressed as a truth table. The next step is to specify an electronic circuit that will act according to the specification given by the truth table. The electrical representation of 0 and 1 depends on having

an electronic device that can be in one of two conditions. The two conditions must be distinguishable, and are often represented by ranges of voltage or ranges of current. For example, two ranges of current flowing in a wire can be defined by specifying a reference value. The value of the current flowing will be above or below this reference current, thus defining two alternative conditions. Similarly, a potential difference between two terminals can be above or below a reference voltage.

There are various agreed standards for logic levels, but we will use a very common one, that used in TTL devices. TTL stands for **transistor-transistor logic** and reflects the internal structure of the TTL family of logic devices. However, we need to concentrate on the voltage levels that are defined within the TTL standard.

The existence of a binary value 0 or 1 at any terminal depends on whether the voltage with respect to a common ground terminal is LOW or HIGH compared with a reference voltage. In TTL the ranges used are 2.0 – 5.0 V for HIGH and 0.0 – 0.8 V for LOW. 3.5 V would be considered HIGH, whereas 0.2 V would be a LOW voltage, but there can be quite a spread of allowed values without affecting the decision about the logic-value intended. This is one of the advantages of digital methods; exact binary decisions between 0 and 1, on which everything depends, do not require exact voltages.

Voltages *outside* the two ranges cannot be interpreted as representing either HIGH or LOW, and should therefore be avoided. If a voltage does occur outside the two ranges, then the result of its application cannot be predicted.

Now that we have a way of representing 0s and 1s with voltages, a block diagram can be drawn for the interlock system which assumes that electrical signals are present, see figure 7.

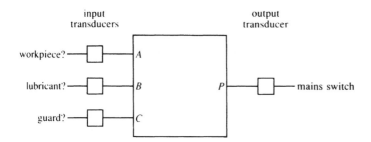

Figure 7: Block diagram for the interlock system

It will also be necessary to find or devise input transducers that produce HIGH or LOW logic levels appropriate to the input conditions. An example of this might be a microswitch that produces an output of 5 V when open and 0 V when closed, as shown in figure 8(a). Similarly, *output* transducers are needed which convert logic levels into appropriate signals to control the interruption of the power circuit to the machine. An example of this might be a relay which closes a circuit when a voltage corresponding to a logic 1 is applied and opens it when a voltage corresponding to a logic 0 is applied, as in figure 8(b).

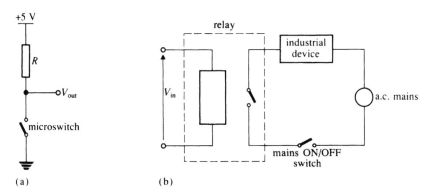

Figure 8: Microswitch and relay

Step 4: Combinational logic devices

Devices that enforce relationships between voltages that can be described in truth tables are available from manufacturers. There are not always devices that meet the precise requirements of an application. However, there are techniques for 'customising' available devices or building up a required function from interconnected devices.

Of the devices that are available, one that might be used is an integrated circuit (IC) on a silicon chip in a plastic or ceramic package. If we use a TTL device the power supply required is 5V +5%. The IC is guaranteed to maintain its specified function when the voltages applied to the inputs of the device are HIGH or LOW as described above; that is, 0.0-0.8 V for LOW and 2.0-5.0 V for HIGH.

For this particular application it is worth checking to see whether a single device is available. It must have (at least) three inputs and one output terminal, corresponding to the logical variables A, B, C and P discussed earlier. The truth table arrived at in Step 2 provides a specification for the required logic device.

Thus, if the device is to implement this truth table, then the application of input voltages corresponding to 1 at terminals A, B and C, respectively, must produce an output voltage corresponding to 1 on P. If the input is changed to any other combination the output must change to 0. This particular form of truth table, where P = *1 only when A and B and C are all* equal to 1, describes the logic function called AND.

Various circuits have been devised which provide this relationship between inputs and outputs. These are called **AND gates** and are made with various numbers of inputs, but have only one output. For an AND gate *all* inputs must represent a 1 to give an output corresponding to a 1, otherwise the output that is generated corresponds to a 0. A three-input AND gate can be represented by the symbol shown in figure 9.

We can therefore use a single three-input AND gate to solve the interlock problem. The resultant system is shown in figure 10.

Figure 9: (AND gate)

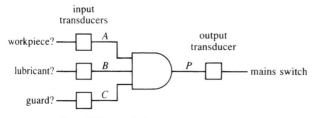

Figure 10:The interlock system

Sequential logic

From counters to coffee machines
The truth table is a complete and systematic statement of a logic problem, which also provides the basis for a practical solution using logic circuits. A certain combination of binary digits appears on the output of a logic circuit whenever a particular combination of binary digits is applied to its inputs, irrespective of the past 'history' of its inputs. In other words, for combinational logic the output depends only on the present input and is not influenced by what has gone before. With this restriction, the solutions can be implemented using combinational logic devices, by devising a suitable arrangement of standard gates.

In sequential logic circuits the inputs and outputs have the form of sequences of binary patterns. The behaviour of a sequential logic circuit is determined not only by its present inputs, but also by its *previous inputs.* The use of the word 'sequence' immediately implies some order in the circuit. Sequential logic circuits can be designed both to modify and to generate sequences of binary patterns. Application examples include the counting of events and the timing of operations for the control of domestic and industrial processes. Two examples will be used to illustrate how sequential systems can be designed.

Electronic counters

Electronic counters find applications in industry and in laboratories whenever a process or experiment involves the registration of individual events; for example, the counting of objects as they pass a particular point on a conveyor belt.

When using electronic counters, the individual events being counted must produce an electrical pulse in order to affect the electronic counter. In the case of the conveyor belt, this could be achieved by passing the objects between a photosensor and a light source. Like its mechanical counterpart, the electronic counter can be reset using an electrical signal from the operator, which forces the output to zero. At any later time the output of the counter indicates the number of events which have occurred since the counter was last reset.

In many applications the output of the counter is used to drive a digital display giving a denary reading of the total number of counts accumulated. Firstly, the case where the total count is provided in the form of a binary code.

Figure 11 shows a block diagram of a simple four-bit binary counter. The input is provided in the form of a series of voltage pulses. The output appears in the form of a four-bit binary word that changes on the arrival of each input pulse.

Let us assume that the counter is initially reset to zero by the operator, which would normally be done by applying a voltage pulse of short duration to the reset input to produce 0000 on the output lines. The output of the counter then changes on the receipt of each input pulse.

In this case the output word changes progressively in accordance with the natural binary code; that is, it follows the sequence:

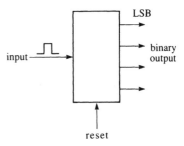

Figure 11: A binary counter

0000, 0001, 0010, and so on up to the maximum count 1111.

As this is a four-bit binary counter it generates a sequence of 16 binary numbers before reaching its limit. After that, it may reset to zero, depending on the application.

You should be able to see why the binary counter is one form of sequential logic circuit. First, the circuit generates a sequence of outputs in response to successive inputs. Secondly, at any stage in the sequence the next output word is uniquely determined by the present output word. Finally, the counter has the ability to 'remember' the effect of an input pulse. This ability sets it clearly apart from the combinational logic circuits.

An automatic coffee dispenser

The counter was an example of a sequential circuit that is so widely used that it has become a standard package that can be bought 'off the shelf'. As an alternative example, look at a circuit that is more likely to be designed and built, as it probably does not exist as a device with all of the necessary requirements.

Figure 12 shows the sort of machine that I have in mind. To get a cup of coffee you have to do two things:

1   Put a cup on the platform underneath the dispenser;

2   Press the 'start' button.

If these two actions are performed in the correct order, the machine will deliver the correct amount of coffee. A third step would be to pay for the coffee. This machine just dispenses the coffee; if payment is necessary it is done elsewhere.

You should be able to see why the coffee dispenser is a sequential machine. One of its inputs is the signal from a sensor on the platform, which indicates the presence of a cup. Another input is the signal indicating that the start button has been pressed. The 'output' of the dispenser is a signal that indicates when to start dispensing coffee and when to stop. Clearly the sequence of outputs depends on the past as well as the present inputs.

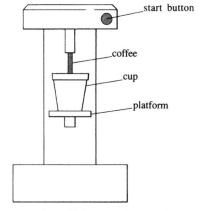

Figure 12: An automatic coffee dispenser

One of the overall design objectives is to ensure that the dispenser is as safe as possible. The main area of concern is to avoid hot coffee being spilled over the person using the dispenser. Can you think of any conditions that have to be satisfied in order to avoid this?

The design of the coffee dispenser

One of the overall objectives of the design will be to make the machine as safe as possible, i.e. it has to avoid pouring hot liquid over everything. Four ways that this could be done are:

*   Do not start dispensing coffee unless there is a cup on the platform.

*   Make sure that the cup is empty.

*   Only dispense a fixed amount of coffee – one cupful.

*   Stop dispensing coffee if the cup is removed at any time.

The simple flow diagram (figure 13) provides a useful stepping-stone to achieving the goal of describing the coffee dispenser in terms of logical 1s and 0s.

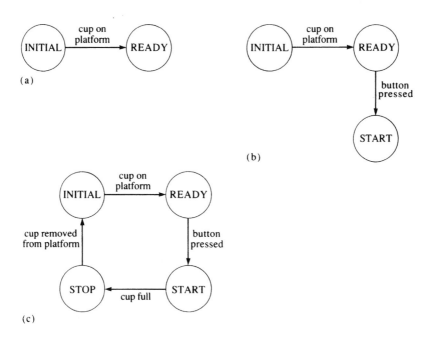

Figure 13: First stage in the design of the coffee dispenser

When the coffee dispenser is first switched on we want it to be in a known state, the 'INITIAL' state. The next stages are to place the cup on the platform and then to press the start button. So we want the coffee machine to move from the 'INITIAL' state to another state when the cup is placed on the platform. We'll call this new state the 'READY' state.

So putting the cup on the platform causes the dispenser to change from its 'INITIAL' state to the 'READY' state. Nothing else will cause it to do that; pressing the start button in the 'INITIAL' state has no effect, as shown in figure 13(b). Pressing the button in the 'READY' state, on the other hand, is all that is needed to cause the machine to change to the next state where it finally dispenses the coffee. I shall call this new state 'START'.

When the correct amount of coffee has been dispensed it should stop, and wait until the cup is removed before starting all over again. So the last state I shall call 'STOP', which is reached when the cup is full, and the state changes to 'INITIAL' again when the cup is removed, as shown in figure 13(c).

This gives us a basic description of the coffee dispenser, showing all of the different states that are required. Notice that I have shown a change when the cup is full, which implies that something will have to test for this condition. So there are three tests in all:

• Is the cup on the platform?

• Has the button been pressed?

• Is the cup full?

Figure 14: Second stage in the design of the coffee dispenser

At this point we shall not worry about how these tests are carried out, but you should be able to see that they are all in a form which has a yes/no answer, which is what we need for a binary logic circuit. The diagram shows what happens if the answer is yes to these tests, for example what happens when the button is pressed, but what happens if the answer is no is not shown. In all cases the machine should stay in the relevant state until the test gives the appropriate response. So while the system is

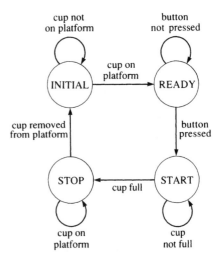

waiting for the button to be pressed, for example, we want it to stay in the 'READY' state. Similarly for the other states, as shown in figure 14.

These extra arrows show that when the indicated condition is true, e.g. 'button not pressed' is true, a state transition takes place on the arrival of a clock pulse, but the state actually stays the same. In other words the state changes to a new state, but that new state is the same as the present one.

This process of successively checking to see whether a particular condition has changed is called **sampling.** Events such as pressing the start button can occur at any time, but we want events to take place only at regular points in time. So to accommodate randomly occurring events they have to be sampled at regular intervals controlled by a clock. Figure 15 shows what happens when a binary signal is sampled.

One thing that should be mentioned now is that whenever sampling occurs, you have to make sure that the clock rate is sufficiently fast to be able to detect the changes in the signal. In the case shown in figure 15, if it were possible to be able to press and release the button in a time that is shorter than the clock period, then the event could go unnoticed.

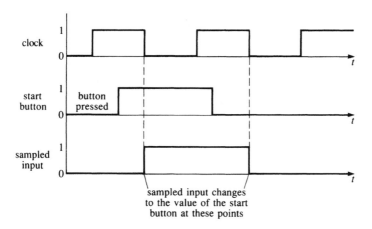

Figure 15: Sampling the signal from the start button

To conclude, we need to know what will happen if an incorrect sequence of events take place, bearing in mind the safety features that we wish to include. The first of these is what happens if you remove the cup when the machine is in the READY state?

Unless we include something extra, it will be possible to press the start button and pour coffee over everything. A suggested solution is to return to the

'INITIAL' state if the cup is removed. Then you would have to replace the cup before pressing the start button has any effect. The second feature is to stop if the cup is removed while dispensing coffee. Going to the 'STOP' state can do this. These are shown in figure 16.

Can you think of any other ways of making the machine dispense coffee when it ought not to? A possible one is to put something other than a cup on the platform so that the machine goes into the 'READY' state. However, this would be unusual.

The next stage is to convert the diagram in figure 16 into one that has letters and numbers rather than words. First the states: instead of calling them 'INITIAL', 'READY', 'START' and 'STOP' they have symbols a, b, c and d, respectively. Next the inputs. These have to have logical variables associated with them A, B and C as follows:

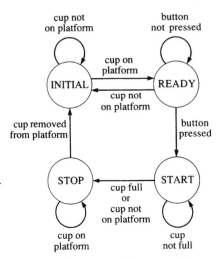

Figure 16: The final functional description of the coffee dispenser

		Yes	No
A	Is the cup on the platform?	1	0
B	Has the button been pressed?	1	0
C	Is the cup full?	1	0

In the actual system we will need to include sensors to produce these binary inputs. The button is probably the easiest to imagine, as it is just a spring-loaded switch. While the button is being pressed the input is 1, and while it is not being pressed the input is 0. The other inputs would need more-sophisticated transducers, such as strain gauges for detecting weight. These input combinations would then have the following meaning:

	A	B	C
No cup on platform	0	-	0
Cup not full	1	-	0
Full cup	1	-	1

Finally there are the outputs. As far as this machine is concerned, there is only one output, which is the signal that tells the machine to start dispensing coffee. The output (P) is

P	Effect
0	Do not dispense coffee
1	Dispense coffee

Binary inputs and outputs

Coding

A single binary input or variable can have only two possible values, 0 or 1. When you have two inputs there are four possible combinations of 0s and is that can be made. For three inputs there are eight possible combinations of 0s and 1s, and so on, each additional input doubling the number of combinations.

How many combinations are possible with 10 inputs?

There would be $2^{10} = 1024$ combinations.

The value of 2^{10} is an important number in the world of digital systems, and as such has been given its own symbol, capital or upper-case K, so 1K = 1024, 2K = 2048, etc. This should not be confused with the standard metric prefix, lower-case k, which equals 1000. You may have come across K in the description of the memory size of computers.

Question 4

Complete this table relating n.2n and K

n	2^n	K
0	1	
1	2	
2	4	
3		
4		
5		
6		
7		
8		
9		
10	1024	1
11		2
12		
13		
14		
15		
16	65536	64

The 2^n different combinations that are possible with n variables can be made to represent some other set of distinct items; for example, the letters of the alphabet or products on sale in a supermarket. This is called **coding**. The 2^n combinations and their interpretations represent the code, whereas the individual combinations represent the code words. Since each of the code words contains a combination of n binary digits or bits, the code is referred to as an n-bit code.

A general rule for binary coding is that the maximum number of distinct items capable of being represented by an n-bit code is 2n. It does not follow that they all have to be used, as you will see in the following activity. However, in the case of a truth table all combinations of 0 and 1 are used because the logical transfer function must be specified for all possible inputs. In some cases all input combinations are possible; in others not all input combinations have an interpretation.

Question 5

What is the minimum number of bits needed to represent the letters 'A' to 'Z' as a binary code?

Number representation

It is sometimes necessary to find a binary code for data that are not already in a binary form. One of the most common examples is numbers. The conversion of familiar denary (base 10) numerals (such as 357, 35700, 3.57 and 0.003 57 to a binary form is commonly required so that they can be handled by a computer.

Natural binary numbers

The normal denary number system uses ten symbols: 0, 1, 2, ... 8, 9.

Symbols are arranged side by side with a 'positional weighting' system which changes their significance (or weight) according to their position. Thus, 397 means 3 hundreds with 9 tens and 7 ones, or $397 = (3 \times 10^2) + (9 \times 10^1) + (7 \times 10^0)$

The significance of the digits is systematically associated with powers of 10. Note that the positions increase in significance from right to left (units, tens, hundreds). The figure on the extreme right is multiplied by 10 to the power of zero, which is 1. The nth from the right is multiplied by 10 to the power of $(n-1)$.

Binary numbers use only two symbols: 0 and 1. The natural binary number system uses the same principle of changing the significance of the digits, but in this case each binary digit, or bit, corresponds to an increasing power of *two*. The interpretation of 101 using the binary number system is: 1 four; no twos and 1 one, or

101 (natural binary) $= (1 \times 2^2) + (0 \times 2^1) + (1 \times 2^0) = 5$ (in denary)

This positional notation can be extended indefinitely, just like the denary system, by adding digits to the left representing 'eights' (2^3), 'sixteens' (2^4), and so on.

The bit at the extreme right (representing 2^0) is known as the **least significant bit** (LSB), and that at the extreme left (representing 2^{n-1} for n bits) the **most significant bit** (MSB). Where it is necessary to avoid confusion, the subscripts 2 and 10 are introduced to indicate natural binary or denary, respectively; for example, 110_2 and 61_{10}.

Binary-coded decimal (bcd) codes

Denary (base 10) numbers of any size can be coded into natural binary form, provided a sufficient number of bits are used. However, there is no clear link between the separate digits of the denary number and the digits of the resultant binary code. You have to do some arithmetic to convert from one to the other. An alternative number system is the *BCD* code (binary-coded decimal), where each denary digit is replaced by a four-bit binary code.

The reason why a four-bit code is used is that there are ten different denary numerals, and four is the smallest number of bits, n, that makes $2^n > 10$. This means that six of the possible 16 values of the four-bit code are redundant. The natural BCD code is also an 8:4:2:1 code, which uses the first ten four-bit natural binary numbers to represent the numerals 0-9.

Note that for denary numbers 0-9, with only one denary digit, the corresponding BCD code has four bits but for denary numbers 10-99, where there are two digits, the BCD code has eight bits. BCD codes require four bits per denary digit. So, for example, to find the BCD code for a denary number, simply take each digit separately, convert it to a four-bit natural binary number, then string the bits together. Some examples are shown.

Denary	Natural binary	8:4:2:1 BCD	
		Tens	Units
0	0000		0000
1	0001		0001
2	0010		0010
3	0011		0011
4	0100		0100
5	0101		0101
6	0110		0110
7	0111		0111
8	1000		1000
9	1001		1001
10	1010	0001	0000
11	1011	0001	0001
12	1100	0001	0010
13	1101	0001	0011
14	1110	0001	0100
15	1111	0001	0101

Denary	Hundreds	Tens	Units	BCD
6			0110	0110
23		0010	0011	00100011
67		0110	0111	01100111
99		1001	1001	10011001
123	0001	0010	0011	000100100011
397	0011	1001	0111	001110010111

Question 6

a) *What are the natural binary and BCD numbers for denary 420?*

b) *What denary numbers would 01101001 represent if it were (i) in natural binary and (ii) in BCD?*

You will have noticed that the BCD equivalent of a large denary number is longer than the corresponding number in natural binary code, but that it is much easier to translate quickly to and from BCD.

Coding for letters and symbols

Another common requirement is to have a code for letters and other characters as well as numbers, so messages can be sent in binary digital form. An important example is *ASCII* (American Standard Code for Information Interchange), used for feeding information into computers from keyboards, operating alphanumeric displays, printers and microprocessors.

The ASCII code uses seven bits to represent $2^n = 128$ characters, consisting of upper- and lower-case letters, numbers, punctuation marks and various standard messages. Some are listed in Table 4.

Table 4

Bits 5 to 7

010	011	100	101	110	111	Bits 1 to 4
SP	0	.	P	,	p	0000
!	1	A	Q	a	q	0001
"	2	B	R	b	r	0010
#	3	C	S	c	s	0011
$	4	D	T	d	t	0100
%	5	E	U	e	u	0101
&	6	F	V	f	V	0110
'	7	G	W	g	w	0111
(	8	H	X	h	x	1000
)	9	I	Y	i	y	1001
*	:	J	Z	j	z	1010
Ü	;	K	[	k	{	1011
'	<	L	\	l	|	1100
–	=	M	]	m	}	1101
"	>	N	^	n	~	1110
/	?	O	_	o	DEL	1111

Logic sub-systems

Devices with one input

Starting with the very simplest case, consider the one-input, one-output combinational logic device shown in figure 1.

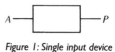

With only one input, there are only two possible input values, so there are two rows in the truth table. The truth tables showing the output of two different devices are:

A	P
0	0
1	1

A	P
0	1
1	0

The first truth table shows that the output is the same as the input, which can be written as $P = A$.

As far as logic levels are concerned, the terminals A and P might as well be connected together by a single wire. However, when the more detailed interconnection properties of logic elements are considered a $P = A$ device is sometimes useful. Its electrical characteristics provide a *buffer* between a source of logic signals having limited power and a further logic device needing more power to drive it than the source can provide. Figure 2 shows the graphical symbol for the buffer, a triangle, which is the same as the standard symbol for an analogue amplifier. We can do this because a buffer is essentially an amplifier with a gain of 1.

Figure 2: Buffer symbol

The second truth table specifies the logic device called the **inverter** or **NOT gate**. Whatever the value of A is (0 or 1), P is always the other binary value (1 or 0). The relationship is referred to either as 'P is NOT A' or as 'P is the inverse of A'.

The graphical symbol for an inverter is shown in figure 3, where it is the small circle that denotes inversion. The triangle is again the standard amplifier symbol, representing the fact that an inverter may also act as a buffer (but with inversion of the output signal).

Figure 3: Inverter symbol

Question 1
What happens when you take the inverse of an already inverted variable, that is, you have an inverter followed by another inverter?

Devices with two inputs
Consider the two-input, one-output device shown in figure 4. With two inputs there are $2^2 = 4$ input combinations or rows in the truth table. The number of different combinations of outputs turns out to be 16.

The first is the **AND** function, taking practical form in the AND gate. In the truth table, shown below, the output is 1 only when *both* input A AND input B are 1.

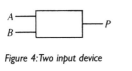

Figure 4: Two input device

A	B	P
0	0	0
0	1	0
1	0	0
1	1	1

The AND gate is specified by the expression P = A AND B. It is graphically symbolised by figure 5.

Figure 5: AND gate

Another important function is the OR function, taking practical form in an **OR** gate. It is defined by the truth table:

A	B	P
0	0	0
0	1	1
1	0	1
1	1	1

It represents a situation such as where an entrance door can be opened ($P = 1$) if either of two security officers, or both, have inserted their personal identifying keys in corresponding locks ($A = 1$ OR $B = 1$ OR both). The output is 1 when any or all of A OR B (OR C, ... if there are more inputs) are 1. It is specified by the expression P = A OR B. It is graphically symbolised by figure 6.

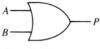

Figure 6: OR gate

[Take care with logic descriptions in words. Some English sentences containing *and* in fact imply the *or* function. If we say 'students and teachers will find this book useful' we mean a reader will find the book useful (P) if the reader is a student (A) OR a teacher (B) OR both.]

Six more of the possible output combinations can be described by a using *AND* or *OR* with inversion.

A	B	P
0	0	1
0	1	1
1	0	1
1	1	0

The first is the inverse of the truth table which we described as the AND relationship, and is called **NAND**, which is short for NOT-AND.

The expression for P in this case is $P = NOT\ (A\ AND\ B)$

A	B	P
0	0	1
0	1	0
1	0	0
1	1	0

The second is the inverse of the truth table which we described as the OR relationship, and is called **NOR**, which is short for NOT-OR.

The expression for P in this second case is $P = NOT\ (A\ OR\ B)$

The graphical symbols for NAND and NOR gates are shown in figure 7. The symbols are basically the same as the ones for AND and OR gates, but with the small circle on the outputs denoting inversion.

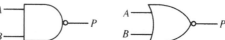

Figure 7: NAND and NOR gates

We are now left with just two more important possibilities. The first is given a special name, **EXCLUSIVE-OR** or XOR, to convey that the output is 1 if A or B but *NOT BOTH* is 1:

A	B	P
0	0	0
0	1	1
1	0	1
1	1	0

The graphical symbol for the XOR gate is shown in figure 8.

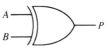

Figure 8: XOR gate

Finally, there is the inverse of the EXCLUSIVE-OR, which is called the **EXCLUSIVE-NOR** or XNOR, which has the truth table:

A	B	P
0	0	1
0	1	0
1	0	0
1	1	1

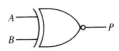

Figure 9: XNOR gate

The graphical symbol for the XNOR gate is shown in figure 9.

It is possible to combine the gates AND, OR and NOT to make other gates. For instance the logic of the XOR can be written:

$P = 1$ only if either $A = 1$ and $B = 0$ or if $A = 0$ and $B = 1$

You can think of this as the output of one AND gate whose inputs are A and B OR the output of another AND gate whose inputs are A and B.

This is shown in figure 10.

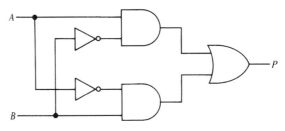

Figure 10: XOR circuit

Question 2

Draw logic block diagrams using AND, OR or NOT gates to describe these control systems:

1   *The exit barrier from a car park is to rise if there is a car waiting to exit and the correct money has been inserted in the coin box.*

2   *The crossing sequence on a pedestrian crossing is to start if the button has been pressed on one side of the road or the other.*

3   *The central-heating boiler is to switch on if the water in the storage tank is cool or if the room temperature is low.*

4   *An automatic watering device in a greenhouse has a pump that will switch on when the soil is dry but not if there is no water in the storage tank.*

5   *An automatic garage door for a disabled driver should open when the car passes through an infrared beam and the car horn is sounded.*

The easiest gate to manufacture is the NAND because of the inverting characteristics of the transistors used in the integrated circuits. In fact any of these gates can be made from a combination of NAND gates. This has a practical advantage when building circuits as typically an integrated circuit chip contains more than one gate (e.g. the 7400 contains 4 two-input NAND gates).

Seven-segment display

A rather more complicated example, which is in widespread use, is the conversion from Binary Coded Decimal to the code needed to generate readable numbers on a seven-segment display. This is the now-familiar pattern used on calculators, voltmeters, clocks and so on. Seven line segments, which can be separately illuminated, can form recognisable denary numbers when they are arranged as in figure 11. Thus, to form the figure 1 it is necessary to illuminate segments b and c, but not a, d, e, f and g. To form 8 it is necessary to illuminate all seven segments.

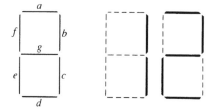

Figure 11: Seven-segment display

A truth table where 1 indicates ON and 0 indicates OFF for the segments can be written as:

Denary digit	Binary code	Segment (ON = 1) a	b	c	d	e	f	g
0	0000	1	1	1	1	1	1	0
1	0001	0	1	1	0	0	0	0
2	0010	1	1	0	1	1	0	1
3	0011	1	1	1	1	0	0	1
4	0100	0	1	1	0	0	1	1
5	0101	1	0	1	1	0	1	1
6	0110	0	0	1	1	1	1	1
7	0111	1	1	1	0	0	0	0
8	1000	1	1	1	1	1	1	1
9	1001	1	1	1	0	0	1	1
No meaning for BCD	1010	x	x	x	x	x	x	x
	1011	x	x	x	x	x	x	x
	1100	x	x	x	x	x	x	x
	1101	x	x	x	x	x	x	x
	1110	x	x	x	x	x	x	x
	1111	x	x	x	x	x	x	x

The new notation, x, in the output columns of this truth tables from row 10 to row 15, represents the *don't care* condition of the output, which indicates that the output can be either 0 or 1. We can assign any value that we wish, because they will never actually be required, as there is no individual BCD code for the numbers 10 to 15. If we wish to display the numbers 10 to 15 (and up to 99) we would need two separate seven-segment digits, each of which will only ever be required to display the numerals 0 to 9.

The way that we can deal with the 'don't cares' would be to set them all to 0. In this way we reduce the number of AND gates that we need to the number of ls in the table.

Question 3

Although designed primarily to display numbers, the seven-segment display can also produce some recognisable letters. Assign values to the don't care terms in the 'segment' columns of the above truth table to provide a display of the six letters ABCDEF (used in hexadecimal notation to represent the numbers 10 to 15) like this:

Why would these, together with the ten BCD digits, not provide a satisfactory display?

ABCDEF

Although the seven-segment display could be built with AND gates, fortunately there is an existing integrated circuit chip that will do the job! The 74LS49 (TTL type) or CD4511B (CMOS type) have five inputs; four for the four binary bits and an additional input that blanks the display.

Practical connection of logic gates

For the purposes of practical connection of logic gates in combination, we will look at the electrical characteristics of the 74LS00 (Quad two-input NAND IC). This is a TTL (Transistor-Transistor Logic) device.

Table I (Extract from data sheet)				
Symbol	Parameter	Minimum	Maximum	Units
V_{CC}	Supply voltage	4.75	5.25	V
I_{IH}	High level input current		20	μA
I_{IL}	Low level input current		-0.36	mA
I_{OH}	High level output current		-0.4	mA
I_{OL}	Low level output current		8	mA

The average current from the supply for this device is 1.6mA. The 7400 is a quad two-input device, which means that it has four separate NAND gates on it. The average current per gate is therefore 0.8mA.

A high logic output current I_{OH} has a maximum value of -0.4 mA (outwards flow), whereas a low logic output current I_{OL} has a maximum value of 8mA (inwards flow). On the inputs to the gates, the high logic input current I_{IH} can be as much as 20μA (inwards flow), and the low logic input current I_{IL} is -0.36mA (outwards flow).

The values of these currents dictate how many gates can be connected to the outputs of other gates, a measure known as the **fan-out** of a gate. Figure 12 shows the output of a NAND gate connected to the inputs of some other NAND gates when the output is a 1 and a 0.

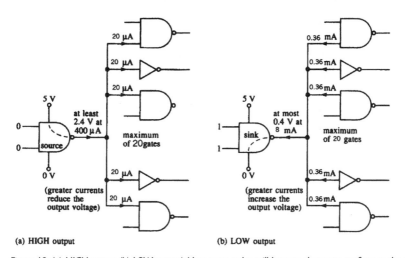

(a) HIGH output   (b) LOW output

Figure 12: (a) HIGH output (b) LOW output) Note some value will have to change to conform to the text

For the 74LS series, when the output is 1, the maximum current (I_{OH}) that is guaranteed to flow is 0.4 mA or 400μA out of the gate. The current is often referred as a **source** current, because it comes from an effective voltage source within the gate. Each of the other connected gates could have an input current, I_{IH} of up to 20μA. Consequently, the maximum number of gates that can be connected to the output of the first NAND gate is 20:

$$\frac{400}{20} = 20$$

Similarly, when the output is low, I_{OL} is at most 8mA, and the input current, I_{IL} required by the other gates can be as much as 0.36mA each. In this case the current flows from the inputs of the other gates into the output of the first NAND gate, so the current is often referred to as a **sink** current. The maximum number of gates that can be supplied by the output of a single NAND gate when the output is low is 22. The fan-out for 74LS series NAND gate is therefore 20 because the lower of the two values is quoted.

In situations where there are unused inputs, such as when you have a three-input NAND gate but a two-input problem, it is common practice to connect the unwanted input to one or other of the voltage rails. If the input were left unconnected the gate would act as if the input were a logic 1, but would be very prone to noise and could often produce spurious results. Manufacturers recommend that for 0 inputs you can connect the gate directly to the 0 V rail, whereas for 1 inputs the gate should be connected to the 5 V rail via a resistor known as a 'pull-up resistor'. A frequently used value is 1 kΩ.

There are a number of different integrated circuit types. The one we have considered is a low power TTL type. The other main type is CMOS (Complementary Metal Oxide Silicon), which is made using Field Effect Transistors and can be sensitive to static charges. CMOS chips work at a range of voltages (between 3 and 15V) and have a fan-out of up to 50 other gates, but are slower than TTL. All unused inputs must be connected to 0V.

Pneumatic systems

The most common place where pneumatics (compressed air) is used is in the pneumatic tyre. A man whose name was Mr Dunlop saw that his daughter was having difficulty pedalling her tricycle with its solid rubber tyres. At this time the motor car was in its infancy and also had solid rubber tyres, luxury horse drawn transport had a solid rubber tyre or a wooden wheel. Farm transport had a steel tyre or hoop on a wooden wheel and some machinery had steel wheels such as steam traction engines and rollers.

Dunlop's early tests consisted of rolling two wheels with his new air filled (pneumatic) tyre. The test was conclusive, the pneumatic tyre travelled to the back wall and rebounded while the solid rubber one just made it about halfway down the yard. This revolutionised road transport and it taken for granted today. The name Dunlop still exists on tyres.

Pneumatics uses air under pressure (typically twice atmospheric pressure in educational equipment). Valves are used to divert the pressure to where it is needed. The main value of pneumatics is that it can work in sensitive atmospheres, where the possibility of electric sparks could be dangerous. Also, the actuators can apply large amounts of force for moving, clamping and pressing.

Pneumatics in everyday life
- Road drills – 'pneumatic drill' is the name you probably use to describe these tools used to dig up roads.

- Automatic doors – the doors on the tube trains and many buses are 'pneumatic', if you listen carefully you will hear air escaping as the door moves.

- Lorry brakes – the braking systems of many large vehicles are 'air assisted', you often hear high pressure air escaping when the brakes are applied.

- Wheel and tyre changing – 'pneumatic' tools are used in tyre fitting bays to undo and tighten wheel nuts as well as to remove old tyres from wheels.

• Dentists drills – next time you are at the dentist you might like to think about the fact that the drill being used is going round at about 500,000 rpm. The best way to achieve this is by using a 'pneumatic' turbine.

Pneumatics in industry

• Paint spraying – pneumatic spraying is used not only for cars and other vehicles, but also for cookers, washers, fridges and many other industrial products.

• Moving components – pneumatic cylinders are ideal for pushing, pulling, clamping and positioning parts ready for further work to be done.

• Punching and pressing – many manufacturing processes use sheet materials (e.g. metal, card, plastic and aluminium foil), these need to be cut out, pressed into shape or folded. Pneumatic cylinders, because they give reliable linear movements, are ideal for these jobs.

Understanding pneumatics

Understanding pneumatics is quite simple, based on an understanding of the operation of a few basic components.

The single acting cylinder S.A.C

Most pneumatic circuits are made up using two basic components – valves and cylinders. The valves control the cylinders, and the cylinders produce force and linear motion to do whatever work is required.

Figure 1 shows a basic pneumatic device – the bicycle pump. If air is blown into the outlet end or the pump, the handle will move to the left. A bicycle pump used in this manner is similar to a single acting cylinder.

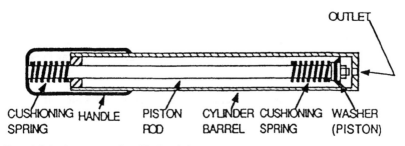

Figure 1: A simple pneumatic device The Bicycle Pump

Figure 2 shows a single acting cylinder

Compressed air is fed into the cylinder barrel. The pressure of the air acting on the surface of a special washer, called a piston, creates a force. The force moves the piston down the cylinder barrel. Attached to the piston is a piston rod which passes through the end of the cylinder barrel. As the piston moves down the cylinder, the piston rod moves out of the end of the cylinder. When the pressure of the air is removed the spring pushes the piston back down the cylinder.

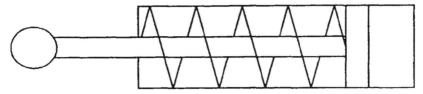

Figure 2: Single Acting Cyclinder

The single acting cylinder is used for light applications where great force is not required and the linear motion is small.

Double Acting Cylinder

A double acting cylinder, shown in figure 3, can be identified in two ways:

1   It has two pipe fittings

2   When you pull the piston rod out and release it, it stays out. There is no spring inside the cylinder to pull the piston rod back in.

Figure 3: Double Acting Cylinder

The 3-Port Valve

When operating a simple single acting cylinder a basic on/off valve cannot be used. This is because once the cylinder is activated and the valve turned off, the piston cannot return because the pressurised air is trapped between the piston and the 'off' valve. In fact an on/off valve (2-Port valve) is only used to control the main air supply to a circuit. To control a single acting cylinder a

3-Port valve must be employed. This valve has one port to which the supply from the compressed air main is connected; a second port to which the cylinder is connected and a third port through which the air in the cylinder can exhaust to the atmosphere when the valve is turned off.

The symbol for the 3-port valve is described below:

The main air supply is represented by the symbol

The exhaust air is represented by ⟶

The cylinder connection is represented by ⎯⎯⎯⎯

When a 3-port valve is 'on', the air flow pattern through it is represented by the symbol:

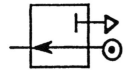

Figure 4

This shows the exhaust route shut off; main air can flow through.

When the 3-port valve is 'off' the air flow pattern through it is represented by the symbol:

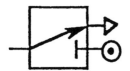

Figure 5

The main air route is shut off; the exhaust air can pass through.

These two symbols are put together to form one flow pattern symbol for a 3-port valve:

The complete symbol is usually drawn showing the 'off' state. Three port valves can be turned on and off by a variety of mechanisms, for example a valve could be turned on by a push button and turned off by a spring. The symbols for these mechanisms are added to the basic flow pattern symbol, as shown in figure 6 opposite.

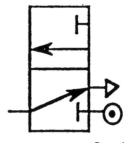

Figure 6

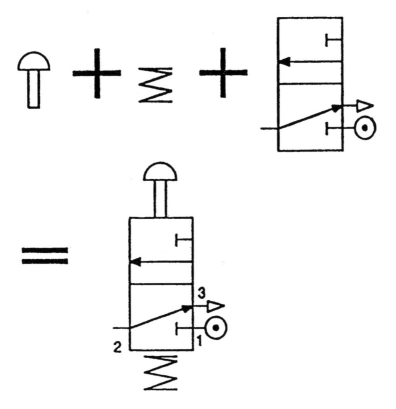

Figure: 7

On most new valves the ports are numbered 1, 2 & 3, as in figure 7, on older valves letters may be used.

Figure 8 shows a 3-port valve system, with the operating button pressed (8a) then released (8b).

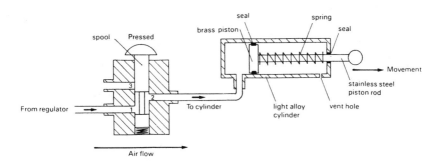

Figure 8a

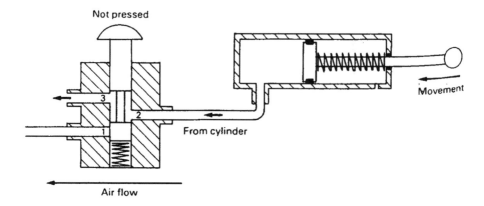

Figure 8b

Five Port Valve

The 5 port valve is commonly used to control a double acting cylinder (DAC). As the name implies, this valve has five ports, as shown in figure 9 opposite.

Notice that a 'lever' symbol appears on both ends of the five port valve symbol. This is rather confusing – there is, of course, only one lever in reality.

Dual Control

Sometimes it is necessary to be able to operate a machine from more than one position. The circuit shown in figure 10 works in this way. The single acting cylinder can be activated by pressing either button A or B.

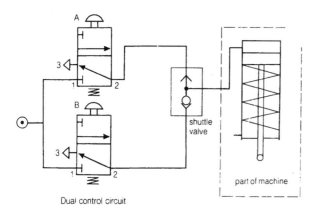

Dual control circuit

Figure 10

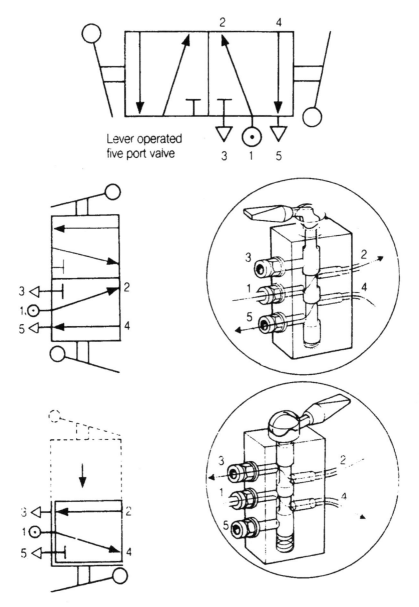

Lever operated
five port valve

Figure 9

The circuit must contain a Shuttle Valve, shown in figure 11.

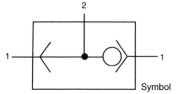 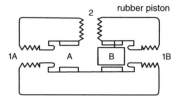

Symbol

Figure 11

A shuttle value has 3 ports and contains a small rubber piston which is free to move A and B within the valve through port 2. Similarly, if air enters the valve through port 1B, the 'piston' is pushed into position A and once again the air can only 'escape' through port 2. If air enters posts, 1A and 1B at the same time, the piston 'floats' between A and B and again air 'escapes' through port 2.

Forces at Work

Air under pressure can be released to do useful work. A single acting cylinder produces a force because air exerts a pressure upon the piston. The force which a piston produces depends on two factors – the air pressure and the surface area of the piston.

If the air pressure was 0.3 N/mm² then the air would exert a force of 0.3 newtons on each square millimetre of piston. So if the piston had a total area if 500mm², then the total force on the piston would be 0.3 x 500 newtons.

Force   = Pressure x Area

Force   = 0.3 x 500

        = 150N

Pneumatic logic circuits

When considering pneumatic logic circuits, the main difference from electrical/electronic logic is that, whereas electrical signals normally flow in one direction, air signals can flow in two directions. This is because the air has to go somewhere when the pressure is released so that the piston can return. All valves therefore are provided with an exhaust port.

Logic with pneumatics: and

A safety system is required for a press-machine so operators do not get their hands trapped when the press closes. Two valves are provided, in a suitable location away from the press, which must both be pushed to operate the machine. In this case the cylinder is single acting, that is, it moves outwards under air pressure and returns by means of a spring. You should be able to see why there have to be exhaust ports on each valve to release the air pressure. These common valves are named 3-port valves (input, output and exhaust). Unfortunately this is not a foolproof system as it can be defeated if the valves are wedged open by weights etc., but it illustrates AND logic.

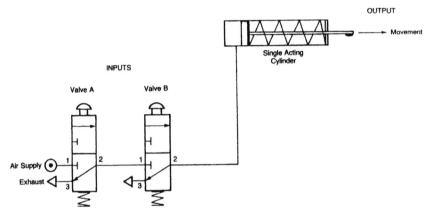

Figure 12: AND pneumatic circuit

Logic with pneumatics: or

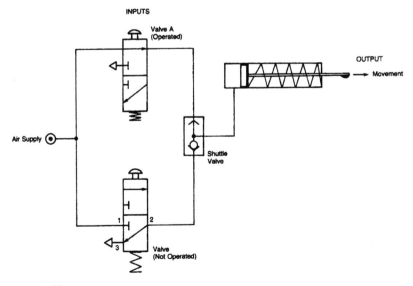

Figure 13: OR pneumatic circuit

A possible design situation is where a door is to be opened from either one side or the other. The problem with this circuit in pneumatics is that the air pressure from one valve operating could leak out through the exhaust port of the other valve. To prevent this a shuttle valve is used; a sort of double acting non-return valve.

Question I

What happens in the OR circuit if both valves are operated together. Consider the action of the shuttle valve.

Another problem with the circuit is that the cylinder is again single acting with a spring return. When either of the valves is released the piston returns and the door closes rapidly! This can partly be improved by restricting the exhaust port outputs to slow the egress of air.

Logic with pneumatics: not

Simply turning the valve upside down will achieve this! In other words the valve is kept open by a spring until it is operated, but there are slightly more elegant ways of achieving this using air operated valves. The air pressure maintains the valve in one position until air pressure is applied (from another 3-port valve) to the opposite end. The constant air pressure must be reduced otherwise the two control pressures would be equal and opposite, preventing the valve from moving. The pressure reduction is achieved with a flow restrictor (analogous with a resistor).

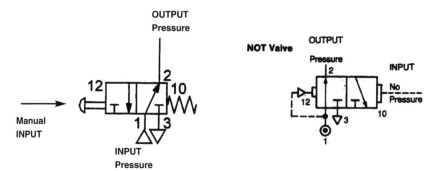

Figure 14: NOT pneumatic circuit

Controlling a double acting cylinder

For a double acting cylinder the power and exhaust paths are switched simultaneously. When the button is pushed the supply at port 1 is connected to port 4 and the outlet port 2 connected to exhaust port 3. The cylinder moves outwards. When the button is released port 1 is connected to port 2 and port 4 connected to port 5. The cylinder moves inwards. Air-operated versions of this valve are available so that other valves working in a logic circuit can operate the cylinder.

In the same way as electronics all these logic elements can be combined. In addition, the actuating cylinders themselves can operate valves automatically as they move.

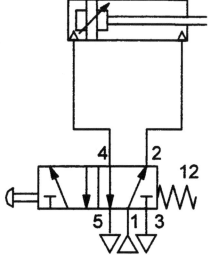

Figure 15: 5/2 valve and double acting cylinder

Pneumatic safety

In a controlled situation pneumatic devices and systems are safe. If they are used incorrectly they can present serious hazards to the user.

To ensure that you work safely, here are some simple guidelines.

• Never point a live airline at yourself or anyone else. Compressed air is very powerful and can cause severe damage to the skin.

• Cover any open cuts on your skin with a plaster. Compressed air can be forced into the skin through an open cut into the blood vessels and cause a similar illness to the 'bends' (as suffered by divers).

• Make sure all pipework is secure.

• Connect all the components in your circuit before switching on the air supply. If you need to alter the circuit, turn off the air supply before making any changes.

• Keep your hands out of the way of moving parts, this will mainly be the pistons and anything attached to them. Compressed air can store a great deal of energy, so pneumatic components can have very powerful movements.

Hydraulic systems

Hydraulic systems are very closely related to pneumatic systems. They both use cylinders to produce linear motion at varying speeds and with varying forces. The basic difference between them is that hydraulic systems use a fluid – hydraulic oil – as a means of transmitting motion and force, instead of the compressed air used by pneumatics. The great advantage of using the liquid is that it cannot be compressed, unlike air. Hydraulic pistons can be stopped at any point in their movement and will stay there whatever happens to the load, whereas pneumatic pistons can only be used safely at the two ends of their movement. In other respects, they operate using the same general principles.

Introduction to basic electronics

Throughout this text you will need to understand standard prefixes, their symbols and meanings. These are:

pico-   (p)   x 10^{-12}

nano-   (n)   x 10^{-9}

micro-   (μA)   x 10^{-6}

milli-   (m)   x 10^{-3}

kilo-   (k)   x 10^{3}

mega-   (M)   x 10^{6}

giga-   (G)   x 10^{9}

Hence

1 microampere (1 μA) = 10^{-6} A

1 kilojoule (1 kJ) = 10^{3} J

1 megohm (1 MΩ) = 10^{6} Ω

1 millivolt (1 mV) = 10^{-3} V

etc.

Electric charge and current

Every piece of matter around us can be thought of as being made up from extremely small basic 'building blocks' called atoms. Each atom is itself a combination of a number of even smaller particles. It has a central nucleus around which revolve particles called electrons. Each electron carries a fixed quantity of electricity, or charge. In many solid materials, particularly metals, although the atoms are firmly fixed in position in the material, the electrons are not all tightly held near the nucleus, and at room temperature large numbers of them are free of their parent atoms and are moving randomly in all directions in the material. These electrons, as well as moving randomly, can be made to flow or *drift* through the material, and this flow of electrons is an electric current. Materials that have large numbers of free electrons are called conductors, the most common being copper.

The labelling of electrons as negatively charged was quite arbitrary, but so also was the designation of the direction of current flow. By convention the direction of current flow is the direction of flow of *positive* charges. However since, in most electrical circuits, electrons carry the charge, the conventional direction of current is opposite to the direction of electron flow. This has no practical consequences, since we shall be concerned with electric currents, rather than with electron motion.

The unit of electric current is the ampere (A). The actual definition is not important here, but a current of 1 A (usually called 'one amp') represents a very large flow rate of electrons, in fact a flow rate of 6.25×10^{18} electrons per second.

Electromotive force and potential difference

Electrons drift through a conductor because:

1   there is a closed path or circuit of conductors around which they can move, and

2   there is, as part of the closed path, a source of *electromotive force* (e.m.f.), which causes a force to be exerted on the free electrons to create the drift.

The most common sources of e.m.f. are batteries and generators. In a battery the e.m.f. is produced as a result of chemical reactions occurring within the battery, while in a generator the e.m.f is produced as a reaction between a magnetic field and a mechanical movement. There are other types of e.m.f. source in which the e.m.f. is the result of supplying heat or light (or both) to suitable materials. One example of such a device is the solar cell used to provide electrical power for artificial satellites, using light from the sun. Some electronic calculators use solar cells instead of batteries to provide the e.m.f required for their operation. Another example is the thermocouple, in which a small e.m.f. is produced by heat applied to the junction of two dissimilar metals. It is used mostly for measuring temperature.

Figure 1 shows the circuit of an electric torch. The torch battery is the source of e.m.f and is connected via copper wires and a switch to the bulb. When the switch is open, no current flows; when the switch is closed, the battery and the conductors form a complete circuit around which current flows.

The units of electronic force are volts (V). When the switch is open, the battery is said to be open circuit, and its e.m.f can be measured as the voltage between its terminals. The actual voltage measured in this way is called the

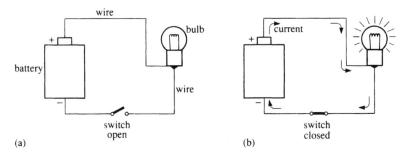

Figure 1: The arrangement of an electric torch: (a) switch open, no current flows; (b) switch closed, current flows

open-circuit voltage, and is not always the same as the *nominal* voltage printed on the battery. A typical torch battery has a nominal voltage of 1.5V, but the open-circuit voltage might be 1.6 V when the battery is new. A car battery (which utilises a different chemical principle) contains six nominally 2 V cells, and has an e.m.f of about 13 volts when fully charged. However, it is nominally a 12 V battery.

The direction of the flow of current in the circuit outside the e.m.f. source is from a higher electrical potential (the + terminal) to a lower electrical potential (the − terminal). We say there is a potential difference between the terminals. The unit of potential difference is again the volt (V). Indeed, the voltage of a battery or other e.m.f. source is another way of referring to its potential difference. It is common practice to refer to the voltage of a source of electromotive force

Electrical energy and power
Returning to the circuit of the torch (figure 1), the flow of current through the bulb causes the tungsten filament inside it to get hot, in fact hot enough to emit visible light. The production of heat is one of the important effects of an electric current.

Chemical energy is taken from the battery and is converted into heat energy in the bulb. The *rate* at which energy is taken from the battery and supplied to the bulb is called the power.

Electrical energy, like other forms of energy, is measured in joules (J) and electrical power is measured in watts (W). One watt is the power needed to generate energy at a rate of 1 joule per second.

The unit of potential difference, the volt, is actually defined in terms of power. It is defined as the potential difference which must exist between two points on a wire to cause a current of 1 A to flow and energy to be dissipated as heat at the rate of 1 watt. The power consumed (in watts) is simply the product of the potential difference (in volts) and the current (in amps) or

$P = V \times I$.

Question 1

a) If a torch bulb is connected to a 1.5V battery and the current flowing in the circuit is 0.2A, what power is dissipated in the circuit?

b) If the four side/tail lights of a car are each rated at 12V, 6W, how much current is being taken from the battery when they are all switched on?

Resistance

The magnitude of the current flowing in a circuit depends on the magnitude of the source of the electromotive force source, and on the device or devices through which the current is flowing. For example, the rear window de-mister on a car has a current of 10 A flowing through it when connected to the 12 V car battery.

If the 12 V battery were replaced with a 6 V battery, the current in the de-mister would be only 5 A. In this case halving the electromotive force causes the current to be halved too. In fact the magnitude of the current is proportional to the e.m.f. source, so that the ratio of voltage to current is a constant. This ratio is called the resistance of the circuit, symbol R, i.e.

$$R = \frac{V}{I} \quad (\text{resistance} = \frac{\text{voltage}}{\text{current}})$$

The unit in which resistance is measured is the ohm (symbol Ω). A resistance of 1Ω will have a current of 1A flowing through it when the potential difference across it is 1V.

Question 2

Work out the resistance of the car de-mister from the information given above.

For many electrical devices, the current is not proportional to the voltage, so that the resistance varies as the current varies. However, devices that have a more or less constant value of resistance over as wide as possible a range of operating conditions are called resistors. A voltage/current graph for a resistor would ideally be a straight line in which the slope of the line is the resistance. Practical resistors have nearly constant resistance and hence an almost linear voltage/current graph.

The physicist Ohm, after whom the unit of resistance is named, was only familiar with materials having a constant resistance when he stated his law that 'the current flowing in an electrical conductor is proportional to the voltage across it at constant temperature'.

The relationship is most frequently written in the form

V = IR

and is commonly given the title '**Ohm's law**'. In fact all it says is that the voltage across a device is equal to the product of the current and resistance. It says nothing about the *constant* nature of R which Ohm's law states.

Conductors are made from materials in which a small potential difference can cause a large current to flow. They thus have very low resistance (or high conductance). Copper is the most commonly encountered conducting material; other examples of good electrical conductors are aluminium, silver, gold and platinum. Notice that all these materials are pure metals. Part of the definition of a metal is that it has large numbers of mobile electrons, and is therefore a good conducting material. Not all conducting materials are necessarily metals, but all metals are conductors.

Insulators are made from materials in which only a very small current flows, even when a very large potential difference exists across them. They have very high resistance and very low conductance. Some examples of common insulating materials are most plastics, rubber, glass and ceramic materials. Air is also an insulating material.

Some materials have neither good insulating properties nor good conducting properties. Examples of such materials are carbon, some metallic alloys and silicon. Silicon is one of the range of materials known as semiconductors, which are used in the manufacture of transistors and integrated circuits.

Resistors
Figure 2 shows the circuit arrangement for the side and tail lights of a motor car. When the switch is closed, the battery must supply current to each of the bulbs. The current flowing through the battery is the *sum* of the individual bulb currents. Each bulb has the full 12 V potential difference of the battery across it. (This assumes that the resistances of the connecting cables and the internal resistance of the battery are sufficiently low that the voltage drops across them are much smaller than the bulb voltages.)

This type of connection of devices is called a **parallel connection**. Figure 3, on the other hand, shows a very different arrangement of light bulbs

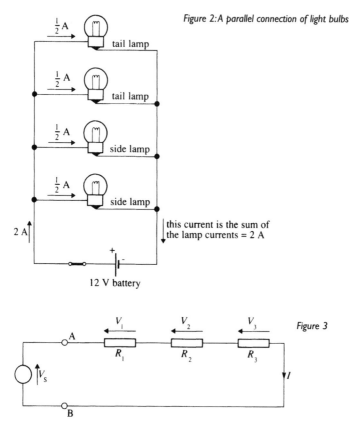

Figure 2: A parallel connection of light bulbs

connected to a source of electromotive force. It shows the arrangement adopted by Christmas tree light manufacturers.

Each of twenty bulbs is connected in **series** across the e.m.f source. With this arrangement the same current flows through the e.m.f. source and through each bulb in the set. Assuming that the internal resistance of the source and the cable resistances can be neglected, the full potential difference of the source is divided up between the individual bulbs. All the bulbs have the same resistance and the potential difference across each bulb is one twentieth of the supply voltage. This type of connection of devices is called a series connection.

Resistors in parallel

Figure 4 shows resistors in parallel, here the current through each resistor is different, but the potential difference across each resistor must be the same because the electromotive force source VS is connected directly across each resistor.

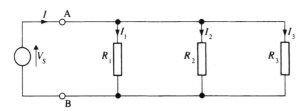

Figure 4: Parallel connection of resistors

Using the relationship $V = IR$ we can write an expression for the current in each resistor:

$$I_1 = \frac{V_s}{R_1} \qquad I_2 = \frac{V_s}{R_2} \qquad I3 = \frac{V_s}{R_3}$$

The e.m.f source supplies all the current in the circuit, so the current I is the sum of the three currents I_1, I_2 and I_3. So:

$$I = \frac{V_s}{R_1} + \frac{V_s}{R_2} + \frac{V_s}{R_3}$$

For the equivalent circuit of figure 4,

$$I = \frac{V_s}{R}$$

Hence,

$$\frac{V_s}{R} = \frac{V_s}{R_1} + \frac{V_s}{R_2} + \frac{V_s}{R_3}$$

and dividing through by V_S gives

$$\frac{1}{R} = \frac{1}{R_1} + \frac{1}{R_2} + \frac{1}{R_3}$$

Rearranging this we get:

$$R = \frac{R_1 x R_2 x R_3}{R_1 + R_2 + R_3}$$

The result we have achieved is that the *equivalent resistance of resistors connected in parallel is equal to the product of the individual resistances divided by their sum.*

Question 3

Work out the equivalent resistance for the three resistors shown in figure 5.

Resistors in series

Figure 6 is a repeat of figure 3, look at the voltages V_1, V_2 and V_3 representing the potential difference across each resistor. The potential at the left-hand end of each resistor is more positive than that at the right-hand end because the current

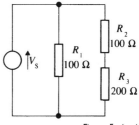

Figure 5: circuit

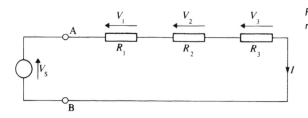

Figure 6: Series connection of resistors

is flowing from left to right. Hence the directions of the arrows representing the polarities of V_1, V_2 and V_3.

The same current I flows through each component in the circuit, so we can evaluate each potential difference using Ohm's relationship.

$$V_1 = IR_1 \qquad V_2 = IR_2 \qquad V_3 = IR_3$$

The total potential difference across all three resistors is $V_1 + V_2 + V_3$ and this must be equal to the applied electromotive force, V_S, since there are no other components in the circuit across which potential can be dropped. (The internal resistance of the source, and the resistances of the connecting cables, can be neglected because they are very much smaller than the resistance values of the resistors.) Hence:

$$V_S = V_1 + V_2 + V_3$$

$$= IR_1 + IR_2 + IR_3$$

$$= I(R_1 + R_2 + R_3)$$

Now in a circuit with one resistor $V_S = IR$

So by comparison the equivalent total resistance is:

$$R = R_1 + R_2 + R_3$$

The result we have achieved is that the *equivalent resistance of resistors connected in series is equal to the sum of the individual resistances.*

The voltage divider

Figure 7 shows a particular case of series connection where only two resistors R_1 and R_2 are connected across the source of electromotive force V_S. We can evaluate V_1 and V_2 in terms of V_S, R_1 and R_2 as follows:

The equivalent resistance of R_1 and R_2 is the sum of their individual resistances, so

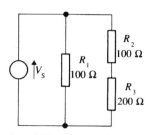

Figure 7: The voltage divider circuit

$$R = R_1 + R_2$$

and

$$\frac{1 x V_S}{R_1 + R_2}$$

but $V_2 = IR_2$

so

$$I \frac{V_1}{R_1} = \frac{V_s}{(R_1 + R_2)}$$

Hence

$$V1 = \frac{V_s}{(R_1} \times \frac{R_2}{R_2)}$$

$$V2 = \frac{V_s}{(R_1} \times \frac{R_2}{R_2)}$$

Dividing one expression by the other gives

$$\frac{V_1}{V_2} = \frac{R_1}{R_2}$$

This expression illustrates the *voltage divider rule, which says the voltage across two resistors in series divides between them in the ratio of their resistances.*

The voltage divider circuit is particularly useful when we need to obtain a potential difference, which is a fraction of the voltage of an applied electromotive force source.

Question 4
In the circuit of figure 8, into what ratio is the voltage divided?

Now work out the values of V_1 and V_2 if the supply voltage is 9V.

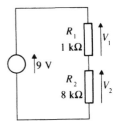

Figure 8: A voltage divider circuit

The variable potential divider
Figure 9 shows several different types of variable potential divider or potentiometer ('pot' for short). A potentiometer is a resistor where the resistance level can be adjusted to a given level.

Figure 9: Several types of variable potential divider

These devices have three terminals, unlike the resistors considered up to now which only have two. Two of the terminals are connected to either end of a resistor. The third, which is called the wiper connection, makes electrical contact with the resistor along its length. Figure 10 shows this in more detail for a potentiometer with a wire-round resistor. As the shaft of the potentiometer is turned, the wiper connection is moved along the length of the resistor.

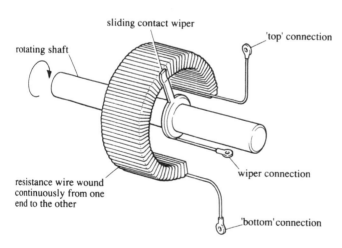

Figure 10: A 'pot' shown in more detail

Activity 1
Obtain a range of different potentiometers and examine their construction. If possible, take them apart to see the resistance and the centre contact (wiper).

The potentiometer circuit can be considered to be part of the voltage divider circuit of figure 7 in which the ratio of R_1 to R_2 can be varied by rotating the shaft of the potentiometer. If a potentiometer is used in a circuit, such as figure 11, adjusting the position of the wiper contact can vary the output voltage. This is useful for providing variable voltage to a bulb or a DC motor for example.

Potentiometers are made with resistors whose resistance varies, in some cases, linearly, and, in other cases, logarithmically along their length, with many different types of resistor and values of resistance. Potentiometers are therefore specified

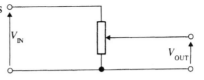

Figure 11: A 'pot' being used to vary the output voltage

with their resistance value, as being LOG or LIN and with the maximum power that they can dissipate. This is important as, being a resistor, they warm up as the current flows through them. They therefore need to get rid of the heat energy.

It is worth stating at this point that real electrical and electronic devices rarely have the exact value that is marked on them. Fixed resistors, for example, may have a tolerance of ±5% (although precision resistors can be as accurate as ±0.1%). This may mean that a 100Ω resistor could have an actual value that lies between 95Ω and 105Ω.

Capacitors
Capacitors can store an electrical charge, and so are often used in timer circuits. There are many different types of capacitor, suitable for different tasks, and made from different materials. They consist of two conducting films, or surfaces, separated by a thin layer of insulation that is often called a dielectric. The dielectric may be flexible, like polythene, in which case the conductor/insulator sandwich can be rolled up so that the capacitor appears cylindrical in shape. Otherwise the dielectric is solid, like mica or ceramic, in which case the capacitor might be a multi-layer pack, as in figure 12(a). In integrated circuits capacitors are usually formed by depositing a layer of

metal on top of the film of silicon dioxide on the surface of silicon, as in figure 12(b), so that the silicon is one of the conductors, and the dioxide is the dielectric.

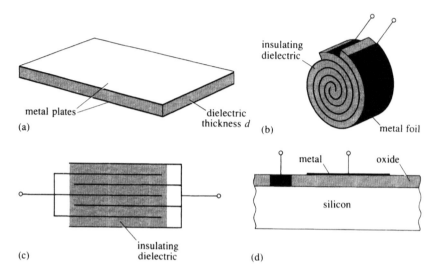

Figure 12: capacitors comprising two conductors separated by an insulator (a) A flat pack capacitor with inter-leaved electrodes. (b) An integrated circuit capacitor with a metal film as one electrode and silicon as the other

When a voltage is applied to the plates of a capacitor, for example by closing the switch in the circuit of figure 13 (below), the battery voltage is transferred to the plates of the capacitor. You might think that this would take place immediately, but it doesn't. To create this potential difference between the capacitor plates, electrons have to be supplied to the more negative plate and removed from the more positive one, and this takes a little time depending on the size of the current carrying the electrons. The electrons supplied to one plate repel electrons from the other, leaving a net positive charge of ionised atoms. Thus a current is required in both halves of the circuit.

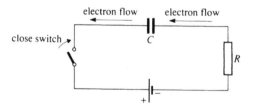

Figure 13: The flow of current as a capacitor is charged up on closing the switch

The unit of capacitance is the farad (symbol F). A more practical unit is the microfarad (μF), or 10^{-6}F. The capacitance associated with integrated circuits are likely to be measured in picofarads (pF), which are 10^{-12} F, or in fractions of a picofarad.

Now, as already indicated, supplying electrons to one plate and repelling or displacing them from the other, as in figure 13, implies that a current is flowing towards one plate and away from the other. Indeed these currents continue to flow at a decreasing rate until the voltage across the capacitor has become equal to the battery voltage and the current has fallen to zero. But since the currents in the two halves of the circuit are the same, the flow of electrons is just as if a current were *actually* flowing round the circuit, despite the presence of the insulating layer in the capacitor. The flow of electrons towards one plate and away from the other, as in figure 13, is indistinguishable in the rest of the circuit from a current flowing round the circuit, except that current only flows when the voltage across the capacitor is *changing.*

If the voltage source in the circuit is an AC *voltage* instead of a DC one, so that the voltage across the capacitor is changing continuously, a corresponding, continuously changing AC current will *apparently* flow through the capacitor. This apparent current is called the *displacement current*, and even though there may be a perfect insulator separating the two plates of the capacitor, it is helpful to think of this alternating current actually flowing around the AC circuit as a whole.

Because there is a time taken to charge and discharge a capacitor, this component is extremely useful in circuits where timing is required.

Inductors
An inductor is a coil of wire like that illustrated in figure 14a.

A varying current flowing through the wire of the coil induces a voltage between the ends of the coil by the process of *electromagnetic induction,* so that a voltage-current relationship is set up which has nothing to do with the resistance of the wire. The voltage between the ends of the coil is

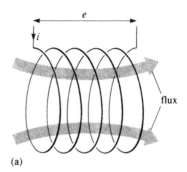

Figure 14a. The magnetic effect of an electric current: (a) the magnetic field in a coil created by the flow of current through the coil

(a)

dependent on the *rate of change* of the current through it and on the number of turns of wire in the coil. It does not depend on the actual value of the current. The electromagnetic principles can be summarised as follows:

1 An electric current creates a magnetic field similar to that produced by a magnet. This magnetic field encircles the wire that carries the current, as shown in figure 14b.

The rings drawn round the wire in this figure are intended to indicate the existence of the field. The arrows show its direction for the current shown; reverse the current and you reverse the direction of the field. The closeness of the lines indicates the strength of the field. The field decreases with distance from the wire. When a current-carrying wire is coiled up as in figure 14a, the field is concentrated within the coil, each turn adding to the strength of the field.

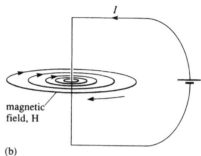

(b)

Figure 14b: The magnetic effect of an electric current: (b) the magnetic field created by the current in a single straight wire

2 This magnetic field produces magnetic flux that follows the *direction* of the field, but the *magnitude* of the flux depends on the material surrounding the wire. The flux per unit cross-section depends on a property called the *permeability* of the material through which the field passes. The relative permeability of most materials is close to 1, but there is one class of materials, the ferromagnetic materials, which have permeabilities of 1000 or more. Ferromagnetic materials include iron, steel and various oxides of iron called *ferrite*. Because of its high permeability the flux produced in a ferromagnetic material by a given magnetic field is much larger than the flux produced in air, even though the magnetic field is the same in both cases.

3 A *changing* magnetic flux induces an electrical voltage, or e.m.f. in a wire placed in this field. The magnitude of the electromotive force (emf) can be calculated from Faraday's law, which states that *the induced e.m.f. in a wire is equal to the rate of change of flux linked with the wire.* So, returning to figure 14a again, a current flowing in the coil will create a magnetic flux through the coil as indicated by the broad arrows. If the current through the coil is now varied in magnitude, the flux will vary correspondingly, with the result that an electromotive force will be induced in the coil itself. This process is called self induction.

The unit of inductance is the henry (symbol H). Thus the inductance of a coil is 1H, if an electromotive force of 1V is induced in it when the rate of change of current through it is 1A per second. The inductance of a coil depends upon the number of turns in the coil and the nature of the magnetic path. For a tightly wound coil, whose diameter is much greater than its length, the inductance is *proportional to the square of the number of turns*. The inductance is greatly increased by giving the coil a ferromagnetic core, as illustrated in figures 14c and 14d. The greatest effect is achieved if the coil and the core encircle each other as shown.

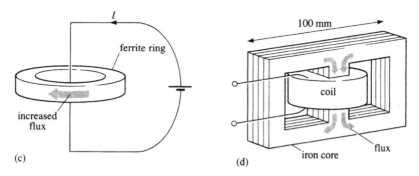

Figure 14c and d: The magnetic effect of an electric current: (c) the same magnetic field applied to a ring of ferromagnetic material produces much more magnetic flux than it produces in air; (d) the structure of an inductor of several henries inductance. The coil and ferromagnetic core surround each other

All conductors possess some inductance, even straight wires. A 10mm length of wire in air has an inductance of the order of 10^{-9} H (1nH). This is significant for telephone transmission lines.

In normal circuits, *an inductor tends to maintain the existing current through it unchanged.* Its behaviour is analogous to that of inertia in mechanical systems. Just as it is difficult to change the rate of rotation of a flywheel abruptly unless you apply a powerful force, so it is difficult to change the current through an inductor abruptly unless you apply a large electromotive force.

The complementary effect is illustrated rather dramatically when the current is switched off in the circuit of figure 15. When the switch is closed the current soon settles to the value of $\dfrac{V_s}{R}$

Then on opening the switch the current abruptly ceases. So what happens? A very large voltage is developed by electromagnetic induction across the coil, so large in fact that a spark may well leap across the air gap of the switch just as it opens. This is the principle behind the creation of sparks by the ignition coil in an petrol engine, where the switch is the contact breaker.

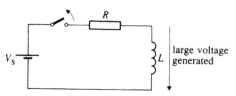

Figure 15:When the current through an inductor is abruptly switched off a large e.m.f. is generated

The importance of induction can also be seen in motors and generators. A DC motor converts electrical current to mechanical rotation by producing a magnetic field in the moving coil that opposes a permanent magnetic field. A DC generator produces electricity because a coil rotates in a magnetic field, which induces a current. In fact some small permanent magnet motors can also operate as generators.

Activity 2

If possible, obtain a small electric motor and take it apart if necessary to identify the coil and magnet components. How is the current transmitted to the moving coil?

Transistors

The key property of transistors that makes them so important is that, like the vacuum tubes that preceded them, they are active devices. That is they are capable of providing signal power gain. The other devices, resistors, capacitors and inductors, are called passive devices.

Transistors are made by forming n- and p-type regions close together in a single crystal of silicon. Adding certain impurities to pure silicon produces these two types. To produce n-type silicon the impurities are chosen such that they release mobile electrons into the crystal to conduct electricity, whilst to produce p-type silicon the impurities are chosen to release mobile carriers that carry positive charges and are called holes.

There are two main types of transistor: the **bipolar** transistor, and the **field-effect** transistor of which MOSFETs are the most widely used type (MOSFET is short for 'Metal-Oxide-Silicon Field Effect Transistor').

Bipolar transistors consist of two p-n junctions placed back to back as indicated diagrammatically in the cross-section diagrams of Figures 16(a) and (b). In n-p-n transistors the p-region is in the middle of the sandwich, whilst in p-n-p ones the n-region is in the middle. These figures also show the corresponding graphical symbols used to represent them in circuit diagrams.

The three terminals, and the regions of silicon, to which they are connected, are called emitter, base and collector. In the graphical symbol the emitter is indicated by an arrow that points in the direction of easy flow of conventional current through the emitter-base p-n junction. So, with n-p-n transistors the arrow points away from the emitter whilst in p-n-p transistors it points towards the emitter. The input voltage to the device is applied between the base and emitter terminals. Varying this voltage causes the current flowing between emitter and collector to vary in response.

Figures 17(a) and (b) show cross-section diagrams of the two complementary types of MOSFET. Here the two p-n junctions are placed side by side at the surface of the silicon, which is then covered by a very thin layer of silicon dioxide. Current flows between the two p-n junctions through a 'channel' formed just under the oxide. In the n-channel MOSFET of figure 17(a) the channel is composed of electrons near the surface of the p-type substrate, whilst in p-channel MOSFETs (figure 17(b)) the current is carried by a channel of holes near the surface of the n-type substrate. The controlling terminal of a MOSFET is connected to a metal film deposited on the oxide covering the channel, as shown. The three terminals, corresponding to emitter, base and collector in the bipolar device, are called **source**, **gate** and **drain** in a MOSFET. The voltage applied between gate and source controls the flow of current between source and drain.

The main practical difference resulting from these complementary forms of each type of device is that the normal DC supplies to them have opposite polarities. For example, with an n-p-n transistor the collector and base are both normally made positive with respect to the emitter; with p-n-p transistors they are both normally made negative. Similarly, with most n-channel MOSFETs the drain and gate

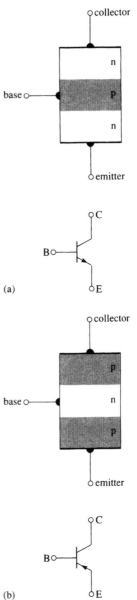

Figure 16 (Diagrammatic cross-sections and graphical symbols of: (a) an n-p-n bipolar transistor; (b) a p-n-p bipolar transistor)

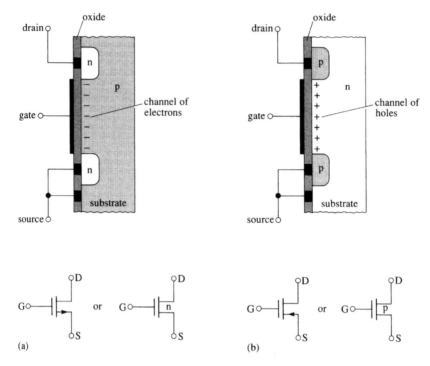

Figure 17: Diagrammatic cross-sections and graphical symbols of: (a) a n—channel MOSFET; (b) a p-channel MOSFET

are normally made positive with respect to the source, whilst with p-channel devices they are made negative.

The essence of the operation of transistors is illustrated in figure 18. Figure 18(a) shows an n-p-n transistor with a few volts applied between collector and emitter and about 0.65V applied between base and emitter. The latter is the DC voltage needed to forward bias the emitter-base p-n junction and it causes electrons to flow from the emitter region into the base region.

Contrary to what you might expect, however, nearly all these electrons will flow on into the collector region, as indicated in the diagram, rather than through the base lead. The ratio of collector current I_C to base current I_B in figure 18 is called the DC current gain of the device, and is usually between about 50 and 500.

Notice that conventional current flows in the opposite direction to the flow of electrons; it is essential, however, to think of n-p-n transistor operation in terms of electron flow. It is the *flow of electrons* from the emitter that divides

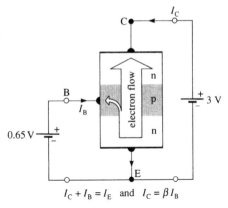

Figure 18: The flow of electrons (and conventional current) through an n-p-n transistor showing how most of the electrons from the emitter flow through the base region into the collector region

$$I_C + I_B = I_E \quad \text{and} \quad I_C = \beta I_B$$

in the base region; about 99 per cent going on to the collector and only about 1 per cent flowing out through the base terminal. It is not helpful when considering how n-p-n bipolar transistors work to think of the flow of current from the collector and the base connections combining in the base region to form the emitter current, although this is how it is represented in circuit diagrams showing conventional DC currents.

The essence of the operation of an n-channel MOSFET is illustrated in figure 19. The gate, the insulator and the substrate behave like a capacitor, so that when a positive voltage is applied between the gate and source a layer or 'channel' of electrons is *induced* in the silicon substrate just under the oxide. The positive voltage applied to the gate attracts the electrons towards the silicon surface and holds them there, bridging the gap between source and drain. When a voltage is now applied between the drain and the source the electrons in the channel are drawn towards the drain and create a drain-source current. As these channel electrons flow away into the drain they must be continuously replaced by electrons drawn from the source, since the number of electrons held under the gate remains the same and is determined by the

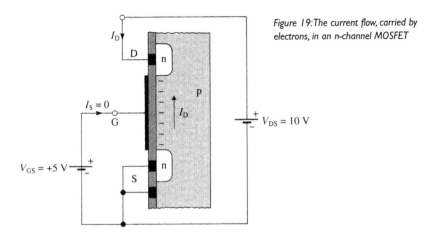

Figure 19: The current flow, carried by electrons, in an n-channel MOSFET

gate-source voltage. Variations in the gate-source voltage give rise to variations in the number of electrons induced in the channel, and therefore give rise to variations in the drain-source current.

It is the *electric field* in the substrate that creates the channel of electrons, which is why the devices are called 'field effect' transistors.

A bipolar transistor as an amplifier

Consider the device shown in figure 20(a). It has an input pair of terminals and an output pair of terminals. In this case one terminal is common to both input and output so it is a three-terminal device. The input pair is connected to a signal source and the output pair is connected to a load, as in figure 20(b). If the average signal power supplied to the load is greater than the average signal power supplied by the input to the device there is signal power gain.

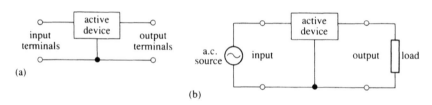

Figure 20 (a:) A representation of a three-terminal device, such as a transistor, as a 'black box'. (b) The device is called an active device if it is capable of delivering more signal power to a load than has to be supplied to its input

For power gain to be possible there must of course be an additional supply of power to the device – not shown in the figure – from which the signal power gain is derived. This is common in a number of energy transformation systems. A transistor requires a DC voltage source and it converts some of this DC input power into signal power and delivers it at the output of the transistor.

In practice, an active device involves a mechanism by means of which it is possible for the input voltage or current to control the DC current flowing through the device. The process is analogous to the way in which the handle on a water tap controls the flow of water through the tap, except that in transistors the 'handle' is an input voltage.

Because active devices such as transistors require a DC supply in order to provide signal power gain, it is necessary to consider both the DC currents and voltages applied to the device as well as the signal currents and voltages. For example, consider the simple circuit of figure 21, which shows a bipolar transistor, connected to a battery via two resistors. The input to the transistor is connected to a signal source via a capacitor because this allows the AC component to pass.

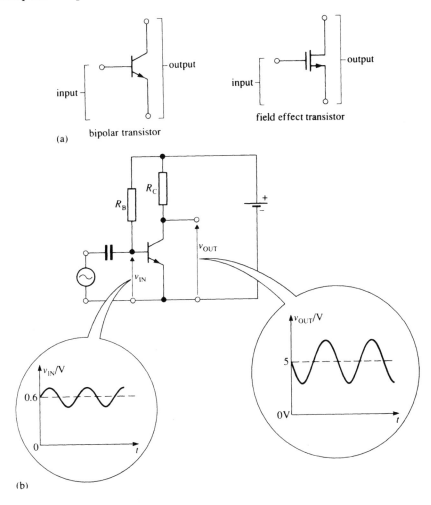

(a) bipolar transistor

field effect transistor

(b)

Figure 21: A simple amplifying circuit using a bipolar transistor. The input and output voltage waveforms are also shown. In each case the varying component of the waveform is superimposed on a DC voltage bias. The 'voltage gain' refers only to the ratio of the amplitudes of the varying components of the output and input voltages

Notice the voltage waveforms at the input and output of the transistor; they both consist of the sum of a DC and an AC component, in other words the AC waveform varies about a DC value. The DC values shown are typical for a bipolar transistor. The *activity* of the device however is concerned with the *varying* or *AC components* of these waveforms. In this case it is convenient to specify *voltage gain* to describe the activity of the transistor because the waveforms shown are voltage waveforms. In the diagram the amplitude of the varying component is larger at the output than at the input so the magnitude of the voltage gain is greater than 1. The voltage gain is defined as the ratio of the *change* in output voltage to the *change* in input voltage.

The resistors in figure 21 are the means by which the DC supply may be connected to the terminals of the transistor and they also play a part in the transistor's AC performance. The value of the voltage gain is always dependent on the DC levels applied to the device because they determine the *operating point* of the device. If the input waveform varied around zero volts, only the top half of the waveform would be seen at the output.

The common – emitter amplifier

The transistor is often found connected as a common emitter device. There are other configurations, but this is the simplest to understand. Calculations are made in this section to determine the DC operating conditions to enable the transistor to work as an amplifier.

The DC components of the circuit of a simple common-emitter amplifier are shown in figure 22(a). To amplify, this circuit is connected to a signal voltage source and to a load R_L by capacitors as shown in figure 22(b).

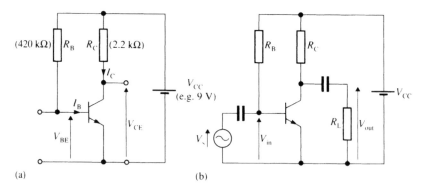

(a)   (b)

Figure 22:The simple common-emitter amplifier circuit with components appropriate for a transistor whose voltage gain is 100, operating at a collector current of 2mA

The first task is to choose the resistors in the DC circuit so that a suitable operating point is set up, that is, to establish appropriate values of V_{CE}, I_C, I_B and V_{BE}.

1   *Collector-emitter voltage* V_{CE}. To allow the collector voltage to vary
    about its operating point in response to the input signal, an operating
    value of V_{CE} of about half V_{CC} is usually chosen: about 4.5 V in this
    example. This allows the largest possible output signal amplitude on
    either side of the operating point without 'clipping' occurring. If the DC
    operating point is set too high the 'top' of the waveform can be cut off if
    it exceeds V_{CC}. Similarly the 'bottom' can be cut off if the DC operating
    point is too low. Obviously both 'ends' are clipped if the signal amplitude
    is too large.

2   *Collector current* I_C. The operating collector current chosen usually
    depends on the output required of the circuit. In this example there are no
    output requirements specified so the choice is an arbitrary one. A DC
    collector current of 2mA has been chosen (though any current from
    10µA to 10mA might be appropriate for a small transistor.) This fixes the
    value of the collector resistance R_C at 2.2 kΩ (i.e. the 4.5V voltage drop
    across it divided by 2mA).

3   *Base current* I_B. To obtain the specified collector current, an appropriate
    input to the base must be provided. In figure 22(a) the base current is
    provided through R_B, which results in the required V_{BE} value of about
    0.65 V appearing across the emitter-base p-n junction. The base current
    needed depends on the current gain of the transistor. So if gain = 100
    then in this case

$$I_B = \frac{2mA}{100}$$
$$= 20\mu A.$$
$$1_B = \frac{Vcc-Vbe}{Rb}$$

Since V_{BE} varies by only a few tens of millivolts from one transistor to
another, it is usually accurate enough to assume a value of 0.65V for V_{BE} in
this equation. So in this case

$$20uA = \frac{9v - 0.65V}{Rb}$$

giving $R_B \cong 420$ kΩ.

Thus the DC operating point of the transistor in this circuit is established as
$I_C = 2mA$, $V_{CE} \cong 4.5V$, $I_B = 20\mu A$ and $V_{BE} \cong 0.65V$.

One of the main problems with bipolar transistor circuit design is making
allowance for the wide spread of gain values. Typically they may be anything
from 100 to 400 or more, so designing for a particular value is only

satisfactory if the transistors to be used are very carefully selected. A similar problem arises with MOSFETs, where the spread is in values of threshold voltage and I_{DSS}.

The transistor as a threshold switch

Combining a voltage divider with a transistor enables resistive sensors like the Light Dependent Resistor (LDR) or the Thermistor (temperature sensitive resistor) to control other devices. One of the two resistors in the voltage divider is the sensor. The value of the other resistor is chosen so that the transistor can be switched on or off by the variation of the sensor. The base-emitter voltage for forward bias is 0.65V.

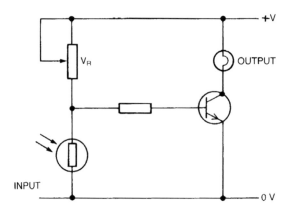

Figure 23: LDR in voltage divider connected to transistor

Figure 23 shows a typical transistor circuit with an LDR. In dark conditions the LDR has a resistance of 100kΩ and the minimum resistance when illuminated for switching on the transistor is 5kΩ. The calculation is shown to find the value of the other resistor when the supply voltage is 9V.

Using: $\dfrac{V1}{V2} = \dfrac{R1}{R2}$

At threshold conditions:

$$\frac{9 - 0.65}{0.65} = \frac{5000}{R2}$$

$$R_2 = \frac{5000 \times 0.65}{8.35}$$

$$= 389Ω \text{ (the nearest practical resistor would be 390Ω)}$$

In practice, a variable resistor may be used so that the actual threshold conditions can be used, but the above calculation would give an approximate value as a starting point. A typical value for a variable resistor in this circuit might be 1kΩ.

Any resistive device can be used in a similar way. For example, a thermistor to sense changes in temperature, a rotary or linear potentiometer to sense change in position and the resistance of a liquid to sense its presence.

Question 5
In order to construct a fire alarm a thermistor sensor will be used to switch on a transistor. The thermistor has a resistance of 1kΩ at 25°C and 100Ω at 100°C. Calculate the value of the other resistor in the voltage divider so that the transistor is just switched on. A 9V battery will be used in a circuit similar to the LDR above.

The operational amplifier

A very important type of amplifier is the operational amplifier (or 'op amp'). It differs from the transistor amplifier in that it has a differential input, and its output is always centred on zero volts. It is represented in diagrams by the triangular symbol shown in figure 24. This diagram also shows the differential input terminals, to which an input signal voltage v_{in} is applied, and the output terminal whose output signal voltage v_{out} is referenced from the zero voltage line. The DC supplies are shown by dotted lines as a reminder that they are needed. Typically they might be + 9 V and – 9 V relative to the 0 V line, and they obviously set limits to the possible voltage swing at the output. With these supplies a peak-to-peak output swing of perhaps 15 V might be possible. Normally these DC connections are not shown in circuit diagrams. So long as the specified DC supplies are connected you can forget about them!

With this device the input voltage is applied between two input terminals *neither* of which is the common or zero voltage line. Thus the input voltage to the amplifier is the *difference* between the two instantaneous input voltages v_a and v_b. It does

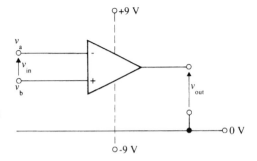

Figure 24: The symbol for an operational amplifier, showing the differential input. Dashed lines show the connections to the DC supplies; they are usually omitted from circuit

not matter what their actual DC voltage is with respect to the zero voltage line, it is the voltage difference between them that is amplified by the amplifier. This is what is meant by a differential input. The voltage gain of the amplifier is therefore given by

$$\frac{\text{output signal voltage}}{\text{differential input signal voltage}}$$

Typically in an operational amplifier the differential gain is 100 000 or more.

Since the output is referred to the zero voltage line it should be 0V when the differential input voltage is zero (e.g. if the two input terminals are connected together). In practice this may require an initial adjustment called the offset adjustment, but as the design of operational amplifiers improves this is becoming less and less necessary.

In the following sections all these annoying details about connecting DC supplies, offsets and the decrease of gain at high frequencies will be ignored. The op amp's most important properties (at low frequencies) are:

1   It has a pair of differential input terminals. One input is called the inverting input and is labelled with a minus sign. The amplified output is inverted with respect to this input. The other input is called the non-inverting input and is labelled with a plus sign.

2   The output voltage is referenced to 0V, so the DC output voltage is zero when the input terminals are connected together or have the same signal input.

3   It has a large differential voltage gain (usually greater than 10^5) at low frequencies.

4   It has a high input resistance between the two input terminals (usually greater than 200kΩ).

5   It has a small output resistance (usually less than 1 kΩ).

Feedback and operational amplifiers

One reason why operational amplifiers are so widely used is that they can easily be converted into different kinds of amplifiers by the use of feedback, namely the connection of the output of an amplifier to its own input by some kind of circuit.

In amplifier circuits the output should be a multiple of the input, so in a 'feedback amplifier' the input is compared, instant by instant, with an attenuated version of the output. The difference between the two is then applied to the amplifier in such a way that the error is reduced. For example, if the intended gain is 100 the input is compared with 1/100th of the output and if there is a difference, a correcting signal is applied to the amplifier.

In practice, in designing negative-feedback amplifiers, an amplifier with far too much gain, such as an op amp, is used, and feedback in the form of resistors is used to reduce this gain to the required value. You might think that this would be a pretty stupid thing to do. Why have the extra gain in the first place, if you are only going to reduce it? True, it does lower the gain, but in exchange it also improves other characteristics, most notably distortion and noise, linearity, flatness of frequency response and predictability.

A basic non-inverting feedback amplifier

Figure 25 shows the basic design of a non-inverting feedback amplifier. It consists of an op amp with a potential divider, consisting of R_1 and R_2, connected across the op amp's output. The output from this potential divider is connected to the *inverting* input as shown. The input signal voltage v_{in} is connected between the *non-inverting* input and 0V line. To understand how this circuit works it is first necessary to understand that the differential voltage $v_a - v_b$ must be extremely small.

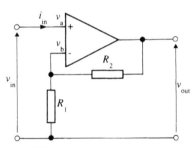

Figure 25: The circuit of a basic non-inverting amplifier

At low frequencies the open-loop voltage gain of the op amp is very large, perhaps even a million or more. This means that if the maximum voltage swing of the output voltage is to be no more than a few volts, then the *differential* input voltage to the op amp, namely $v_a - v_b$, must be no more than a few *microvolts*. In other words v_a and v_b must be at *very nearly the same signal voltage*.

Suppose the overall feedback amplifier is to have a voltage gain of 100 and an output signal amplitude of; say, 5V. Then the input signal amplitude v_{in} between the non-inverting input and 0V must be

$$\frac{5V}{100} = 50mV,$$ of which $v_a - v_b$ contributes only a *few microvolts*.

So the input voltage is almost entirely the voltage drop across R_1. The output voltage is obviously the voltage drop across R_1 and R_2 in series, so the voltage gain G of the whole circuit, ignoring $v_a - v_b$, is given by

$$G = \frac{Vout}{Vin} = \frac{R1 + R2}{R1}$$

G is called the *closed-loop voltage gain* of the circuit, and is determined almost entirely by the feedback circuit. It is hardly affected by small changes in open-loop gain.

The circuit adjusts itself to maintain this value of G as follows. Suppose the output increases a little for some reason; this will cause the voltage drop across R_1 to increase a little. But a small increase in the voltage drop across R1 results in a proportionately much larger reduction in $v_a - v_b$, which causes a corresponding rapid decrease in the output voltage, bringing it back to where it should be.

A basic inverting amplifier with feedback

Figure 26 shows an alternative design of negative feedback amplifier based on an operational amplifier. In this circuit the output is an inverted-and amplified-version of the input waveform. Again two resistors R_1 and R_2 are added to the op amp, but in quite a different configuration. How does it operate?

The first thing to remember is that the input resistance of the op amp is high – over 200 kΩ, for example. If R_1 and R_2 are chosen so that they are much less than the input resistance of the op amp (e.g. no more than a few tens of kilohms) the input current at any instant will flow almost entirely through both R_1 and R_2. Only a negligible current will flow through the inverting input to earth.

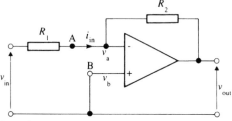

Figure 26:The circuit of a basic inverting feedback amplifier

The next point to remember is that, just as with the non-inverting amplifier, the differential input voltage $v_a - v_b$ must be extremely small; typically no more than a few microvolts. But in this circuit v_b is connected to earth, So v_a is virtually at earth potential. The inverting input of the op amp in this circuit is called a virtual earth. The voltage drop across R_1 is therefore approximately

$$\frac{Vin}{R1} = - \frac{Vout}{R2}$$

Or the closed-loop voltage gain of the circuit becomes

$$G = \frac{Vout}{Vin} = -\frac{R2}{R1}$$

In this circuit, the closed-loop voltage gain is simply the ratio of the two resistors connected to the op amp. The minus sign indicates that the output is inverted.

A summing amplifier

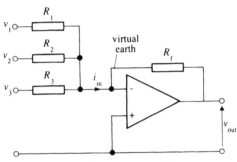

The presence of a virtual earth in the circuit of figure 27 provides a very convenient method of adding voltages together. The formula below shows the method. The total current i_{in} arriving at the virtual earth is clearly the sum of the currents flowing in the three input resistors, thus with $v_a = 0$,

Figure 27: The circuit of a summing amplifier.

$$i_{in} = \frac{V1}{R1} + \frac{V2}{R2} + \frac{V3}{R3}$$

But this current does not go to ground at the virtual earth, it flows on too through R_f,

$$\text{so } i_{in} = \frac{Vout}{R_1}$$

Therefore

$$\frac{V1}{R1} + \frac{V2}{R2} + \frac{V3}{R3} = \frac{Vout}{Rf}$$

So, if all the resistors are of equal value:

$$Vout = -(V1 + V2 + V3)$$

The output voltage is simply minus the sum of the three input voltages. By choosing different values of R_1, R_2 and R_3 it is possible to multiply each input voltage by a factor before adding them together. The virtual earth in this circuit is sometimes called the summing junction.

This summing amplifier is the basis for a simple digital to analogue (D to A) converter.

Diode

Diodes are semiconductor devices that allow the current to flow in one direction only.

The Thyristor

In some ways the thyristor appears similar in its operation to a transistor. The thyristor also has three legs, and when a small current is applied to the gate it causes a large current to flow between anode and cathode. The important difference is that the thyristor will continue passing anode/cathode current even when the small gate current has ceased. This condition is called latching.

Unlike the transistor, whose collector/emitter current is proportional to base current, the thyristor will pass its maximum anode/cathode current when triggered with just a small momentary gate current.

106 is a cheap thyristor that can pass up to 3A between anode and cathode, and it can form the basic of many useful alarm circuits where a switch closing only briefly produces a continuous warning signal. The trigger switch could be a membrane panel (e.g. under a carpet), a reed switch, a tilt switch or several of these wired in parallel so that any one closing, even for a split second, triggers the thyristor into conduction. Water or moisture bridging across two probes will also conduct enough gate current to trigger the thyristor.

Relays and solenoids

A relay is an electrically operated switch. It has two main parts: an electromagnet and a switch. When current is supplied to the coil of the electromagnet, it becomes magnetic and attracts a plate whose movement operates the switch. There is a mechanical, but no electrical, connection between the electromagnet and switch. The switch itself can be of any type, but SPDT and DPDT types are the most common.

The purpose of a relay is to make it possible to switch large currents (sometimes at a high voltage) when only a small control current is available from a circuit. For example, if a large pump needs to be switched on automatically when the water level rises in a cellar, a relay can be used as part of a transistor circuit. Water rising between the two probes causes base current to flow, and thus a larger collector/emitter current flows to energise the relay and switch on the pump-possible operated by mains current.

A solenoid is similar in its operation to an electromagnet, but the coil is wound around a hollow tube rather than a metal core. When current flows through the coil, it becomes magnetic and pulls a metal rod into the tube. This rod is connected to something that needs a mechanical movement. The bolts of some locks, for example, are moved by the action of a solenoid.

The 555 timer

The control input in sequential circuits is usually derived from a central clock or oscillator. The most common device that is used is the 555 timer. Figure 28 shows a block diagram of the 555 timer with the pin numbers of the actual integrated circuit indicated.

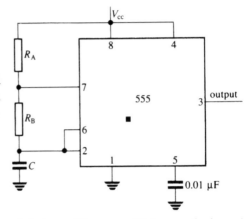

Figure 28: A 555 timer connected up as an oscillator

When it is connected up in this way it behaves like an oscillator, producing an output waveform like that shown in figure 29.

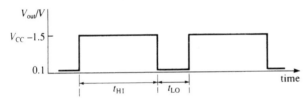

Figure 29: The output from the circuit in Figure 28

The output voltage alternates between a high of $(V_{CC} - 1.5)$ V to a low of 0.1V. The actual value of V_{CC} can be anything from 4.5 to 18 V.

The timing when the outputs are low and high is given by:

$$t_{LOW} = 0.693 \, R_B C$$

$$t_{HI} = 0.693(R_A + R_B)C$$

where R_A, R_B and C refer to the resistors and capacitor in the circuit in figure 28. This means that t_{HI} will always be larger than t_{LOW}

Using these two equations gives the ratio of the timing periods:

$$\frac{t_m}{t_{LOW}} = \frac{R_A + 1}{R_B}$$

Question 6

Choose values for R_A, R_B, C *to produce the waveform shown in figure 30.*

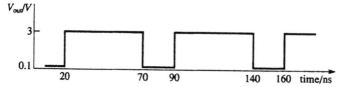

Figure 30: Waveform for question 6

Hint: use the ratio of timing first and choose a sensible value for one resistor; then calculate C by substituting value for R_B.

Note: time is in nano-seconds.

It is clear from the expressions for t_{LOW} and t_{HI} above that it is impossible to produce a symmetrical waveform using this circuit. The only way would be if $R_A = 0$, which would mean that V_{CC} is directly connected to pin 7, which would stop the timer from functioning correctly.

The reason why the two times are different is that in one half of the cycle the capacitor, C, is being charged through resistors R_A and R_B and in the other half the capacitor is discharging though resistor R_A alone. So, if we make $R_A = R_B$, and then arrange it so that R_B is short-circuited when the capacitor is charging, the square wave will be symmetrical. We can do this by placing a diode (assuming that it has zero resistance) across R_B as shown in figure 31.

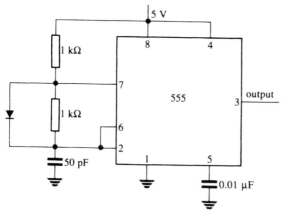

Figure 31: Symmetrical waveform generator

Question 7

Sketch the square-wave output that would be generated by the circuit shown in figure 31. You will only need to calculate one time interval.

Sensors

Resistance change and voltage sensors can be used as part of a potential divider input to a transistor threshold switch or operational amplifier. Digital and current change sensors can also be used with these devices but will need to be in series with a resistor to enable switching from 0V to supply voltage. Inductor and capacitor sensors are more difficult to use and are not dealt with in this publication. Table 1 shows common electronic sensors and their outputs.

Environmental change	Sensor type	Sensor output
Light	Light dependent resistor LDR. Photodiode Phototransistor Photovoltaic cell	Resistance change Current change Current change Voltage
Temperature	Thermistor Thermocouple Bimetallic strip	Resistance change Voltage Movement
Movement – displacement	Potentiometer Inductor (magnet in coil) Variable capacitor Reed switch and magnet Tilt switch Conductive foam	Resistance change Inductance change Capacitance change Digital Digital Resistance change
Movement – strain	Strain gauge	Resistance change
Movement – liquid level	Wire probes Dissimilar metal plates Air plate capacitor Float switch Float potentiometer	Resistance change Voltage Capacitance change Digital Resistance change
Touch	Two metal plates Push switch	Capacitance change Digital
Sound	Microphone	Voltage or capacitance change
Pressure	Diaphragm switch	Digital

Table I Common electronic sensors

Related Websites

Electronics

http://www.chipcenter.com/	Literature and information on microchips
http://www.howstuffworks.com/	Simple explanations of everyday devices
http://www.altera.com/	Literature and information on microchips
http://rswww.com/	RS components (data, prices and orders)
https://catalogue.maplin.co.uk/	Electronic component supplier
http://www.microchip.com/	One-stop information about microchips
http://www.milinst.demon.co.uk/	Milford Instruments (Basic Stamps, Robotics, etc.)
http://www.softronix.com/logic.html	Multimedia Logic (free download of Logic Simulation software
http://www.demon.co.uk/flight/pictrain.htm	Flight Electronics (PIC trainer)
http://www.stampsinclass.com/	Parallax Inc (supplier of Basic Stamp Micro-controller)
http://www.ti.com/	Texas Instruments
http://www.data-harvest.co.uk	PIC system; Control hardware and software
http://www.economatics.co.uk/education	PIC system; Control hardware and software; electronic systems PIC chip control and software

Pneumatics

http://www.pneumatics.com/	General information
http://www.norgren.com/training/	Training pages (PowerPoint) to download. Symbols and circuits etc.

General Control

http://content.honeywell.com/sensing/	Information about industrial and controllers sensors
http://www.tecquip.co.uk/	Equipment and software for training
http://www.bsi.org.uk/education/	British Standards Institution
http://www.unilab.co.uk	Suppliers of educational control equipment

Answers to Questions

Systems

Question 1

System	Inputs	Outputs
Wall switch	movement	electrical current
Volmeyter	electrical current	movement
Washing machine	dirty clothes water detergent electrical energy	clean clothes dirty water waste chemicals waste heat
Bicycle	muscular energy	movement (kinetic energy)

Question 2 *(see opposite)*

Question 3

Open loop sub-system

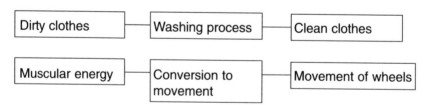

1. central heating with a thermostat

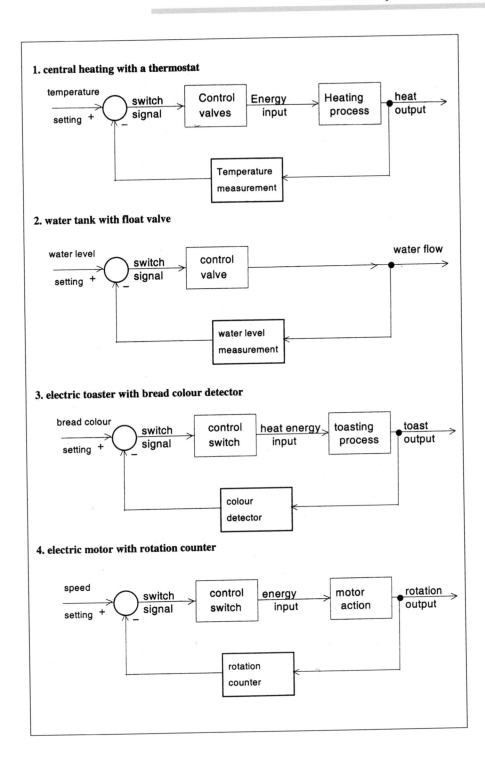

2. water tank with float valve

3. electric toaster with bread colour detector

4. electric motor with rotation counter

Logic Systems

Question I

The safety guard could, for example, close a microswitch (a tiny switch requiring only a small movement to close it) when in position. Then condition C could be expressed as 'Is the microswitch closed?' YES ($C=1$) or NO ($C=0$) or 'What is the state of the microswitch?' CLOSED (1) or OPEN (O) or 'The microswitch is closed. 'TRUE (1) or FALSE (O).

Similar expressions must be found for any other way of specifying that the guard is in position. Similarly, the output requirement can be expressed as 'Does the mains switch turn on the machine/' YES ($P = 1$) or NO ($P = O$) or 'What is the state of the machine when the mains switch is on?' GO (I) or STOP (O) or 'The mains switch turns on the machine.' TRUE (1) or FALSE (O)

Question 2

The mains switch will not turn the machine on ($P = O$) when the workpiece is not in position ($A = O$), there is not adequate lubricant ($B = O$) but the safety guard is in position ($C = 1$).

Question 3

The 16 combinations are listed in the same systematic way that was used for three inputs. You may have found, when you tried to list them that, unless you had some systematic method, it was difficult to remember which combinations you had already found and which, if any, were missing.

A	B	C	D
0	0	0	0
0	0	0	1
0	0	1	0
0	0	1	1
0	1	0	0
0	1	0	1
0	1	1	0
0	1	1	1
1	0	0	0
1	0	0	1

1	0	1	0
1	0	1	1
1	1	0	0
1	1	0	1
1	1	1	0
1	1	1	1

Question 4

Table should look like this

n	2^n
0	1
1	2
2	4
3	8
4	16
5	32
6	64
7	128
8	256
9	512
10	1024 = 1K
11	2048 = 2K
12	4096 = 4K
13	8192 = 8K
14	16384 = 16K
15	32768 = 32K
16	65536 = 64K

Question 5

If we assign a binary code to the letters a-z we will need 26 separate code words. The nearest number that is a power of 2 that is greater than 26 is 32, or 2^5. We therefore need five bits at least, in which case six of the code words will be unused.

Question 6

a) $420 = 256+128+32+4$

$$=2^8+2^7 + (0 \times 2^6) + (0 \times 2^4) + (0 \times 2^3) + 2^2 + (0 \times 2^1) + (0 \times 2^0)$$

= natural binary 110100100

= BCD 0100 0010 0000

b)   Natural binary $= 64 + 32 + 8 + 1 = 105_{10}$

BCD $= 69_{10}$

Logic Sub-systems
Question 1

Inverting twice restores the original value.

If $P = $ NOT A

then $P = $ NOT (NOT A) $= A$

Question 2

See diagrams on page 113.

Question 3

Table of codes for letters A-F

Letter	Code	a	b	c	d	e	f	g
A	1010	1	1	1	0	1	1	1
C	1100	1	0	0	1	1	1	0
D	1101	1	1	1	1	1	1	0
E	1110	1	0	0	1	1	1	1
F	1111	1	0	0	0	1	1	1

This would not give a satisfactory hex display, because 8 and B, and 0 and D would be indistinguishable. A crude solution sometimes adopted is to use lower case b and d for B and D, respectively, but this is still liable to give confusion between b and 6. Practical hex displays use more than seven segments, or a matrix of dots, to provide better symbols.

Pneumatic systems
Question 1
The shuttle valve (depending on its construction) will move to the centre and air may pass both ways. The circuit may operate as EITHER OR BOTH.

Introduction to basic electronics
Question 1
a)   Voltage = 1.5V, current = 0.2A

Power = voltage x current,

power dissipated in this circuit is

1.5 x 0.2 = 0.3 watts

b)   Each bulb is supplied at 12V and dissipate 6W

Current through each bulb is $\dfrac{6}{12} = 0.5A$

Total current is therefore 4 x 0.5 = 2A

Question 2
De-mister voltage is 12V and current is 10A

Resistance $\dfrac{12}{10} = 1.2\Omega$

Question 3
Work out the series resistor equivalence first.

The equivalent resistance of R_2 and R_3 is 100 = 200 = 300Ω

There are now two resistors in parallel (100Ω and 300Ω)

The equivalent resistance of these is $\dfrac{100x300}{100+300} = \dfrac{30000}{400} = 75\Omega$

Question 4

Potential divider so $\dfrac{V1}{V2} = \dfrac{1}{8}$

as $V_1 + V_2 = 9$

then $V_1 = 1V$

and $V_2 = 8V$

Question 5

For switch on at 100°C, $R_1 = 100$, $V_2 = 0.65V$, $V_1 = 9 - 0.65 = 8.35V$

Using the potential divider ratio $R_2 - 100 \; x \; 0.65 \; / \; 8.35 = 7.8\Omega$

Nearest practical resistor 10Ω circuit will switch on slightly below 100°C

Question 6

Figure 30 showed that the voltage goes from 0.1 V to 3 V

The value of 3 V is derived from $3 = Vcc - 1.5$

so $Vcc = 4.5V$

Using the equation in the text, $\dfrac{t_{HI}}{t_{LO}} = \dfrac{50}{20} = 2.5$

So $-\dfrac{R_A}{R_B} = 2.5 - 1$

If we let $R_B = 1 \; K\Omega$, then $R_A = 1.5 \; K\Omega$

Returning to the other equation, we can now substitute R_B to obtain C:

$t_{LO} = 0.693 \; R_B \; C = 20$

$C = 28.86 \; pF$

Question 7

Since $Vcc = 5 \; V$, the waveform will switch between 0.1 and $(5 - 1.5)$ $V = 3.5V$. The time spent in each state will be the same as t_{LO} from the original equations:

$t_{LO} = 0.693 \; RB$

$C = 0.693 \; x \; 1 \; x \; 1000 \; x \; 50 \; x \; 10^{12}$

$s = 34.65ns$

The resultant waveform is shown in the figure.

Diagrams for Question 2 of Logic Sub-systems

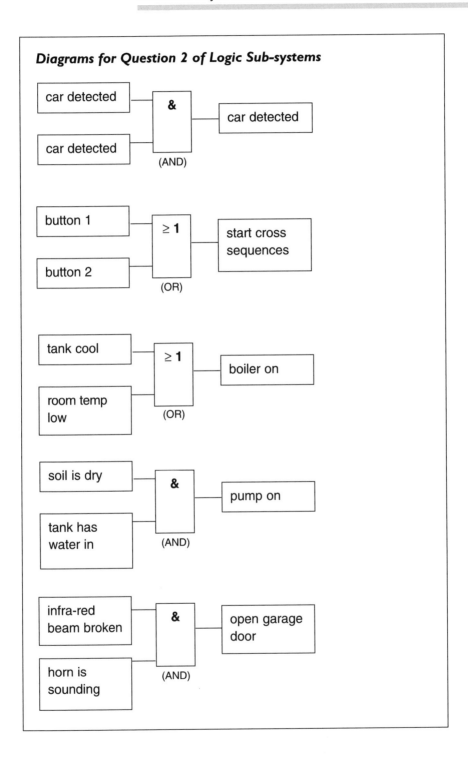